How to Hire Winners – Legally

Laurence Lipsett

HRD Press
Amherst, Massachusetts

First Edition, First Printing

Copyright 1994 © by **HRD Press, Inc.**

All rights reserved under International and Pan-American Copyright Conventions. No part of this book may be reproduced in any form or by any means, electronic or mechanical, including photocopying, without permission in writing from the publisher. All inquiries should be addressed to HRD Press, Inc., 22 Amherst Road, Amherst, MA 01002. Published in the United States by HRD Press, Inc.

ISBN 0-87425-982-7

Production Design by Jack Sanders and Jennifer Hornberger
Cover Design by Old Mill Graphics
Editorial Work by Mike Haley

About the Author

Laurence Lipsett is a consulting industrial psychologist specializing in personnel selection. He has consulted with more than 200 firms, including Xerox, Bausch and Lomb, Quaker Oats, and Corning, Inc. Dr. Lipsett earned a bachelor's degree from the University of Michigan and master's and doctor's degrees from the University of Buffalo. Before he began his private practice he directed a community psychological services center at Rochester Institute of Technology. He has taught at the University of Rochester and was awarded the Chancellor's Award for Excellence in Teaching while employed as a professor of human resource management and industrial psychology at Empire State College of the State University of New York.

Dr. Lipsett is the author of more than 40 articles in professional journals and is the senior author of *Personnel Selection and Recruitment,* published by Allyn and Bacon. He is a licensed psychologist and a Diplomat of the American Board of Professional Psychology.

Disclaimer

The publisher and/or author make no warranties, express or implied, with respect to this book and neither assumes any responsibility for any legal complaint or action occasioned by any following of its guidelines. The user assumes all risk and liability whatsoever in connection with the use of or reliance upon the materials contained herein and there are no oral agreements or understandings or warranties collateral to or affecting the understanding implicit in the purchase of this book.

The book is intended only as a general guide to hiring, is not to be construed as written in accordance with any Federal or State laws, and is not intended to serve as a substitute for legal advice. The practices of the user organization should be tailored to accommodate to the particular need. In case of any uncertainty with respect to any specific organization policy, competent legal counsel should be sought. The individuals portrayed in this book are completely fictional. Any resemblance to real persons, living or dead, is purely coincidental.

TABLE OF CONTENTS

Introduction	ix
Chapter 1.	
How to find the best applicants	**1**
	1
What to look for in employees	8
Where to find the best applicants	15
29 recruiting data bases	19
Refinements in recruiting	20
Legal issues in recruiting	21
Hiring costs	
Chapter 2.	
How to design selective and legal	**23**
application forms	25
The comprehensive application blank	26
Illegal questions	28
Model application for sales position	
Chapter 3.	
How to get the most from application	**37**
forms and résumés	41
Examples of résumé analysis	45
Weighted application blanks	46
Impostors	
Chapter 4.	
How to interview efficiently & legally	**51**
Before the interview	52
Preparing for the selection interview	53
Illegal questions	54
Breaking the ice	55
Information about the company	55
Principles of questioning	56
Employment experience	58
Education	60
Extracurricular activities	62
Personality and motivation	62
Control of the interview	63
The patterned interview	64
Coordinating and training interviewers	66

Chapter 5.

How to spot winners and losers 69

Transcribed interview segments
and interpretations 69
How questions get results 76

Chapter 6.

How to test applicants legally 79

Types of tests 80
Assessment centers 85
Testing with job samples or simulations 87
Legal issues in testing 88
Buying tests 89
Types of test publishers 91

Chapter 7.

How to avoid negligent hiring 93

The importance of checking 93
Lay a foundation for investigation 94
How to check 95
Who should investigate 98
Interviewing individual informants 101
Special problems in investigation 102
Issues in giving information 102

Chapter 8.

How to minimize legal risks in hiring 105

Summary of legal applications, recruiting,
and interviewing 105
The Americans with Disabilities Act of 1990 108
The Civil Rights Act of 1991 114
Hiring decisions 117
Strategies for compliance 118

Chapter 9.

How to make sure you hire winners 123

What can go wrong 123
Organizing for hiring decisions 125
What contributes to hiring decisions 126
Developing selection criteria 127
What to look for in applicants 128
A case study 130
Review of steps in recruiting and selecting 131

Postscript 133
Index 135

Introduction

Developing an effective work force depends on:

1. Determining what employee qualifications are needed.

2. Finding where such employees are located.

3. Attracting their applications.

4. Selecting from the appropriate applicant pool.

5. Orienting new hires into the company culture.

6. Providing initial and ongoing training as needed.

7. Appraising performance and providing coaching as needed.

8. Providing effective supervision.

9. Developing compensation plans that motivate employees and encourage retention.

10. Providing benefits that serve humanitarian needs and encourage retention.

11. Providing career development opportunities.

12. Continually monitoring morale and responding constructively to any problems.

This book deals with recruiting and selection. Following its principles and techniques will result in hiring qualified employees, but they will continue to be effective only if training, supervision, pay, and employee services are also effective.

chapter 1

HOW TO FIND THE BEST APPLICANTS

WHAT TO LOOK FOR IN EMPLOYEES

Job Descriptions

When a business needs additional employees, the first step in staffing is to develop a thorough description of the duties to be performed—a job description. This is commonly expressed in terms of action verbs like sells, computes, assembles, types, operates, manages, etc. To show a job's emphasis on different activities a percentage of time may be noted, e.g., waits on customers 80%; arranges stock 20%. A job description also includes identification of equipment used, such as forklift truck, personal computer, offset press, micrometer, etc.

In a small business the manager may be able to develop an adequate job description from personal knowledge. In larger businesses a job description can be developed by interviewing employees already on the job and their supervisors, inquiring about skills, knowledge, equipment, and responsibilities for product, equipment, money, and other people.

The *Dictionary of Occupational Titles,* available in libraries and from the U.S. Government Printing Office, contains job descriptions for 20,000 representative jobs, based on 75,000 on-site studies. These generic job descriptions provide useful clues, but it is important for each company to make sure that its job descriptions exactly fit its circumstances. Other sources of pre-written job descriptions or position descriptions are also available from private sources that are advertised periodically.

HOW TO HIRE WINNERS — LEGALLY

Job Analysis

A job analysis is a formal procedure for studying jobs. It can be used as a basis for job descriptions, establishing wages and salaries, determining training needs, setting performance standards, and identifying safety hazards. A job analysis schedule, usually completed by a professional, includes a concise job summary, educational requirements, specific vocational preparation, aptitudes, temperaments, interests, physical demands, environmental conditions, experience, licenses, relation to other jobs and workers, equipment used, materials and products involved, and a thorough description of tasks.

Guidelines are provided in the *Handbook for Analyzing Jobs,* available from the U.S. Government Printing office. Fine and Wiley (1977) also provide a useful reference. Several methods of job analysis have been published. All involve obtaining information from incumbents, supervisors, and other experts regarding tasks, working conditions, responsibilities, and requirements. Off-the-shelf guidelines that a non-specialist might be able to use are provided in the *Position Analysis Questionnaire* (1969).

For ordinary business circumstances, a formal job analysis is not required. However, it can be an important factor in a lawsuit regarding discrimination in hiring, promotion, or layoff. It may be also be a factor in union negotiations. To be prepared for possible litigation, it is prudent to have some kind of job analysis available.

Person Specifications

A job description, by itself, suggests, but does not spell out, skills, knowledge, and personal characteristics required in a recruit. These items can be derived from a job analysis or from less formal procedures. Examples include knowledge of particular programming languages, ability to lift 50 pounds, reading engineering drawings, shift work, and working in heat or cold. Licenses and certificates are absolute requirements in some occupations.

Employers often prefer to hire persons who already have relevant experience, as in selling, operating machine tools, and managing, and desired experience can be specified. Personal characteristics are critical in some jobs. For example, effective sales-

2

HOW TO FIND THE BEST APPLICANTS

persons have persistence, and managers need organizing ability. Creativity is important in some advertising and research jobs.

Educational requirements, like a B.S. or a high school diploma, have often been specified, but government EEO regulations apply. It is legal to specify requirements for graduate degrees for college teachers because they are involved in the degree granting process. However, the specification of a particular degree may be interpreted as discriminatory, because it may eliminate a disproportionate number of minorities or women. Many advertisements that specify degrees contrary to government policy can still be seen because the government is not monitoring this activity closely, but a recruiter would be safer at least to add the words "or equivalent" to any advertisement mentioning a college degree. Even more appropriate and less subject to legal challenge would be task-oriented expressions like "ability to write creative advertising copy" or "experience with CAD/CAM."

Recruiters have specified college degrees as a simple way of identifying a certain level of intellectual development, but Xerox successfully recruited English engineers who did not have American-style B.S. degrees. The practical "engineer" who developed the extrusion process used in plastic garbage bags did not have a degree. The person who carried the title of "chief engineer" at Fisher-Price Toys for many years grew up with the manufacturing process and was fully effective without a degree.

The success or failure of present and former employees is one of the best sources of information about person specifications. What kinds of people have succeeded? What kinds have failed? In this analysis, however, it is important to differentiate the relevant characteristics from the irrelevant ones. For example, did a salesman succeed because he was tall or because he was persistent? Did a manager succeed because subordinates liked her or because she organized effectively?

Technically, a "job" is a group of tasks. "Carpenter" and "Plumber" are jobs, and many people may hold the same job in this sense. A "Position" is a group of tasks performed by a single individual in a particular place. The next page includes a representative position description and person specifications.

HOW TO HIRE WINNERS — LEGALLY

POSITION DESCRIPTION

Secretary to Vice President, Marketing

General Responsibilities: Prepares correspondence, sorts mail, schedules appointments, answers telephone, maintains department files, and performs other office duties as directed.

Specific Responsibilities:

1. Schedules appointments and meetings, following general or specific instructions from supervisor.
2. Transcribes machine dictation.
3. Composes and prepares selected correspondence as directed.
4. Answers telephone, exercising judgment regarding:
   a. Offering an immediate response.
   b. Forwarding call directly to vice president.
   c. Taking a message to avoid interrupting vice president.
   d. Forwarding call to another department.
5. Places outgoing calls as requested by vice president.
6. Opens and routes non-personal mail.
7. Schedules appointments and meetings for vice president. Maintains vice-president's appointment calendar.
8. Greets visitors, ascertains nature of business, conducts or directs them to appropriate person or dismisses them.
9. Makes travel arrangements on request.
10. Compiles sales reports.
11. Keeps minutes of meetings.
12. Copies documents on copy machine.
13. Maintains confidential files on department personnel.
14. Maintains files of correspondence, sales, and advertising.
15. Supervises one clerk/word processor.
16. Performs other duties as directed.

HOW TO FIND THE BEST APPLICANTS

PERSON SPECIFICATIONS

Education: Prefer two years of college; high school or equivalent essential.

Experience: At least three years business office experience. Prefer familiarity with marketing and sales functions.

Skills: Keyboard speed at least 50 wpm; experience on at least one word processing system.

Personal: Skills in oral and written communication at least at the two-year college level. Ability to maintain courteous and professional demeanor in personal and telephone contacts. Mature judgment in answering, routing, or dismissing visitors and telephone callers. Ability to maintain confidentiality. Ability to supervise clerk/word processor, exercising judgment and consideration regarding training, amount and quality of work assignments, and daily interaction.

SOME QUESTIONS TO BE ANSWERED IN PREPARING POSITION DESCRIPTIONS

I. What the worker does, how he/she does it, why it is done?
What are the factors that distinguish this job from other jobs?
What is the basic function, e.g., inspection of machine parts; marking photographic paper, etc.?

II. What objects, materials, tools, or equipment are used?
What is the value of the equipment used?
What is the scope of independent judgment or decision-making?
Set up or maintain any machines?
What records are kept and how are they kept?
What reports are prepared?
To what extent does the worker make estimates or order supplies?

III. What physical activities are required: lifting, pulling, carrying, reaching, etc.?

IV. What is the work environment (hot, cold, ventilated, etc.)?

V. Number and type of subordinates supervised: hiring authority, performance appraisal, discipline, discharge, etc.?

HOW TO HIRE WINNERS — LEGALLY

VI. What are the "essential functions" of the job in the event that it is necessary to accommodate an applicant with a disability? (see explanation below)

The Americans With Disabilities Act of 1990 requires new attention to person specifications in regard to physical and mental disabilities. The law prohibits discrimination against a disabled applicant if that person is able to perform the "essential functions" of a job. For example, it is legal to require a certain keyboard speed where the job requires spending a major amount of work time at a keyboard. On the other hand, if a secretary is expected to drive a car for an occasional errand, having a driver's license probably would not be regarded as an essential function. Prudent employers will review their job descriptions to identify "essential functions" to prepare for extending job opportunities to the disabled and to provide defenses in the event of legal challenge.

The 1990 law also requires "reasonable accommodation" in hiring the disabled if that does not involve "undue hardship" on the employer. No definitions of those phrases are offered. More details on this law are offered in Chapter 8.

In the position description for Secretary to Vice President, Marketing, a section on *Essential Functions* might be added, as follows:

1. Keyboard speed at least 50 wpm.
2. Ability to transcribe machine dictation.
3. Telephone skills at the level of an executive secretary.
4. Filing skills, both alphabetical and numerical.
5. Ability to maintain confidentiality.
6. Professional demeanor.

Perhaps the following responsibilities could be omitted: Composing correspondence; handling mail; making travel arrangements; compiling sales reports, using copier, and supervising.

6

HOW TO FIND THE BEST APPLICANTS

SOME QUESTIONS TO BE ANSWERED IN PREPARING PERSON SPECIFICATIONS

I. *Experience Requirements, if any.* Many production and clerical positions require no previous experience. Experience may be required, however, for supervision or independent responsibility as a professional or journeyman.

II. *Education, Knowledge, Skills.* Except for licensing or certification, no jobs require specific degrees or diplomas, although employers of engineers, accountants, etc. have found it convenient to specify degrees. The phrase "or equivalent" may reduce the possibility of a lawsuit, but requirements can be stated in terms of certain mathematical proficiency, ability to read and understand labor regulations, level of written and oral communication, knowledge of tax accounting, etc.

III. *Physical Demands.* Include amount and frequency of lifting, standing, walking, bending, kneeling, sitting, reaching, withstanding temperature changes, travel, driving, telephoning, visual acuity for reading gauges, rotating shifts, irregular hours, etc.

IV. *Personality Requirements.* Is the work routine or varied? What are the internal and external contacts? What are the extent and type of relationships? What is the nature of the supervisory responsibility, if any? What management style is expected in this company? What is the responsibility for independent planning and responsibility? What are the requirements in regard to initiative, creativity, organizing ability, etc.?

V. *Are Your Person Specifications Legal?* A recent study conducted by the Bureau of National Affairs found that 19 percent of employers now refuse to hire smokers or give preference to nonsmokers. Some employers have been known to deny employment to obese people, motorcycle riders, and others with lifestyles disapproved by the employer. It is legal and probably desirable to maintain a smoke-free workplace, but it may not be legal to reject applicants who smoke off the job. At the time of this writing in 1993, 24 states have some type of "privacy law" that prohibits discrimination on the basis of private pursuits so long as job performance is satisfactory.

HOW TO HIRE WINNERS — LEGALLY

WHERE TO FIND THE BEST APPLICANTS

Job Posting

In your own backyard is a good place to start recruiting to fill new vacancies. Promotion from within contributes to company morale, and in any organization there is a chance that a current employee will be able and willing to fill a new vacancy. Under optimum conditions a company will have a human resource inventory in its computer, so that people with skills like word processing, statistics, or supervision can be identified. We don't know of many companies with such a system, but there is another way— job posting.

Aside from the practical value of posting job openings, companies with government contracts are *required* to "make job openings known to all employees." Some union contracts also require posting jobs in the bargaining unit.

Companies have resisted posting because they wanted to avoid a flood of unqualified applicants or because they wanted to fill jobs on a political basis. Posting does not eliminate politics in an organization, but it does open the system for everyone, including the government, to see what is going on. The number of unqualified applicants can be minimized through accurate person specifications. Any applicant who does not meet all the specified qualifications can be eliminated quickly.

When employees in an organization know that there are vacancies they will tell their friends and relatives whether there is posting or not. One advantage of this is that recruiting costs are minimized. Another advantage is that people recruited by current employees are more likely to resemble people who are already successful employees. A disadvantage is nepotism; another is that cliques can develop. In times of labor shortage some firms have found it useful to pay bonuses to employees for recruits they bring in. In times of labor shortage sign-on bonuses may be paid to employees recruited from any source.

Networking

A majority of desirable jobs are filled through networking. Many employees belong to fraternal, civic, and religious organizations, and they serve on boards of not-for-profit organizations.

HOW TO FIND THE BEST APPLICANTS

Human resource professionals, purchasing agents, engineers, salespersons, chemists, and other professionals attend local and national meetings. When they talk business over dinner or lunch, job openings are often mentioned. Acquaintance in these organizations may enable members to identify the most effective workers. An employment manager can use these networking connections to invite members of any outside groups to recommend acquaintances. This not only saves advertising dollars; it also reaches potential recruits who are not currently reading help wanted ads.

Walk-ins

At the employment office of any large company walk-ins arrive on their own in the hope that they can be hired for some job. Many low-skill and clerical jobs can be completely filled by walk-ins. But that does not yield the best labor force. Organizations that want to develop a full applicant pool continue to advertise, visit schools, and use agencies no matter how many applicants walk in unsolicited.

Responding to walk-ins is another problem to consider. If they are not needed today, they might be needed at some future time. Or their acquaintances might be better qualified. One acceptable practice is to allow any walk-in to complete a short application form designed for screening and keep it on file for a limited period. Any person coming to an organization deserves a considerate reception, not only for humanitarian reasons but also for the self-interest of the organization's public relations.

Advertising

When employee ranks are not filled through informal and inexpensive sources, local newspaper help wanted advertisements are used by 85 percent of employers, according to a survey by the Administrative Management Society. Classified ads have been useful in recruiting secretaries, machine operators, and others in the more common occupations. An ad with the minimum number of words may attract a sufficient number of applicants when the labor supply is ample. On the other hand, a more complete description of requirements can save the recruiter's time by weeding out some unqualified applicants. If the salary is firm, it saves time to state it, but in many cases it will be negotiable. Blind ads may save a recruiter's time because public relations do

HOW TO HIRE WINNERS — LEGALLY

not have to be considered. However, more applicants respond to ads that include the company name.

Display ads provide more opportunity to sell the job, to attract the best applicants regardless of labor market conditions. Creativity is important in times of labor shortage, and an example of a creative display ad is presented below. Principles of creativity in advertising include: identifying the interests and concerns of the target group; including something that will catch attention quickly (visual in print or auditory on radio); and highlighting the points that appeal to the target group.

The advertisement for a "sales veteran" does not pretend to be creative, but it sharply targets mature people with sales experience who understand the conditions described. It is "blind" partly because the company is small and unknown to the public and partly because the president wants to avoid phone calls and walk-ins. This ad pulled 30 responses in a medium-sized city where the unemployment rate was about four percent. About half of the respondents were basically qualified.

For some jobs advertising in local shopping guides can be just as productive as in a metropolitan daily, and it is cheaper. Advertising directed to a national labor pool can be placed in the *New York Times,* the *Wall Street Journal,* and the *National Business Employment Weekly. National Ad Search,* P.O. Box 2083, Milwaukee, WI 53201-2083, compiles ad listings from major newspapers. There is also a TV Job Search Network, based at 1650 Tyson Blvd., Suite 570, McLean, VA 22102.

A firm named SRDS offers for sale *The Recruitment Solution,* which profiles more than 3,500 recruitment advertising opportunities, including newspapers, business publications, trade shows, conventions, and job fairs. Call 1-800-851-SRDS.

In the spring of 1993 the Career Television Network (TCTN) began broadcasting on CNBC, the cable television outlet of the National Broadcasting System. In addition to listing job openings the program provides information about the employer's geographical area, including neighborhoods, schools, and recreation. Interviews with people currently employed by the company bring out advantages of working for that employer.

HOW TO FIND THE BEST APPLICANTS

Job applicants respond directly to TCTN, which sends each one a questionnaire that is scanned and then rated for skill experience and any criteria furnished by the employer.

As this is written the program is aired for one hour in the early morning, in some areas as early at 5:00 A.M., but TCTN claims many responses despite the hour. The network hopes to increase programming hours. Located near Chicago, TCTN can be reached at (708) 505-8300.

Most employment advertising is placed by managers or human resource professionals. For more difficult or more unusual advertising projects, however, it may be cost-effective to employ an advertising agency. Many agencies are satisfactory, but some specialize in recruitment advertising. Recruitment advertising agencies with the most offices are listed below.

Austin Knight Advertising: Offices in Toronto, Montreal, Chicago, Boston, New York City, Sausalito, CA.

USA TODAY'S CAREERS publishes recruitment advertising every Tuesday in the Money section. 1-800-872-3433.

Berkeley Placement Service: Offices in New York City, Hicksville and Westchester, NY, Waldwick, West Paterson, and Woodbridge in New Jersey.

Bernard Hodes Advertising: Offices in Tempe, AZ, Irvine, CA, Encino, CA, Palo Alto, CA, Denver, Fort Lauderdale, Atlanta, Chicago, New York City, Philadelphia, Dallas, Houston, Arlington, VA, Cambridge, MA.

Thompson Recruitment Advertising: Offices in Phoenix, Los Angeles, Denver, Philadelphia, Seattle, West Allis, WI, San Mateo, CA, Farmington, CT, Independence, OH.

One-office agencies specializing in recruiting are available in many cities.

In any contact with an advertising agency it is important to determine the company's needs and objectives. Cost of advertising can be weighed against the proposed salary of the recruit, the difficulty of attracting qualified applicants, and the cost of settling for a less-than-satisfactory employee. Before an agency

HOW TO HIRE WINNERS — LEGALLY

is paid a fee, it is possible to obtain a proposal that may include samples and a cost-benefit analysis of different media.

A decision to advertise involves considerations of the time required by someone to screen applications and conduct screening interviews. A way to reduce (but not eliminate) this problem is to use employment agencies.

Employment Agencies

The public Job Service (the name differs in some states) is free for both applicants and employers, and in fact listing there is *required* for firms with government contracts. In some instances the Job Service may be able to refer applicants whose skills have been tested with the General Aptitude Test Battery.

Some employers feel that they receive more individual attention from private employment agencies, and about half of employers use them. For professional jobs the employer commonly pays the fee, but the agency pays the cost of advertising and screening. However, any agency, public or private, seeks to place the maximum number of applicants; they are not interested in eliminating applicants. Thus it is important for an employer to clarify the job description and the person specifications provided for the agency. It is also important to be firm in insisting that the agency refer only candidates who clearly meet the specifications. Continuing communication between employer and agency is required for effective use of agencies.

Educational Institutions

For entry-level jobs in occupations like secretarial work, engineering, data processing, and accounting it is economical to go directly to the placement offices of schools and colleges. With enough advance preparation interviews can be arranged on campus, with no fee involved. As in the case of agencies, recruiting in educational institutions is most effective when there is a full measure of two-way communication. Companies often leave descriptive brochures in the placement office. The placement officer will usually cooperate in referring students who meet the specifications that are clearly spelled out.

HOW TO FIND THE BEST APPLICANTS

Professional Organizations

The potential applicant pool for many professions is national or even international. The professional journals of most professions carry recruiting ads that can be productive. The publications of trade associations likewise carry employment advertising. Conventions of many organizations include a placement service, where both applicants and employers can register and make connections for interviews. Recruiting through professional organizations, however, takes time. The lead time to place an ad in a journal may be several months, and conventions are commonly held once a year.

Job Fairs

Job fairs have a relatively low cost per hire. Following substantial local advertising, one organization or several may rent space large enough to accommodate a number of interviewing spaces where interviewers spend all day screening applicants. Local organizations like chambers of commerce sometimes conduct job fairs.

Senior Citizens

The diminishing pool of younger workers has led some organizations to recruit older workers. One-quarter of the reservationists for Day's Inns are now senior citizens. Substantial numbers of seniors are employed by Kentucky Fried Chicken, banks, and a home improvement chain, which has found that customers welcome the opportunity to be waited on by a retired plumber or carpenter. The American Association for Retired Persons sponsors the National Older Workers Information Service (NOWIS) to provide employers with information about employment of older workers. The address is AARP Worker Equity Department, 1909 K Street, N.W., Washington, DC 20049.

Military

Retired military personnel constitute another fruitful labor pool, which may be particularly useful for companies with military contracts. Some military retirees can be recruited through local sources, but specialized agencies include the Military Recruiting Institute in Atlanta and the Retired Officers Association in Alexandria, VA.

HOW TO HIRE WINNERS — LEGALLY

Geographical Approaches

Areas of high unemployment can be recruiting sources for some jobs. One security guard firm advertised in a county a two-hour drive from their area of operation. After screening by telephone, they offered paid lodging in their city and scheduled workers for two consecutive days off. They were able to fill their ranks with an ample supply of qualified guards.

Another geographical adjustment to recruiting is to move the business to an area of high unemployment, in an inner city or a depressed area anywhere.

Outplacement

The downsizing of American industrial firms has caused the development of widespread activity in outplacement. AT&T, General Motors, Stroh's, and many others have operated their own outplacement services, where job announcements by firms in a hiring mode are welcome. Most metropolitan areas have offices of outplacement firms that would like to hear from recruiters.

Executive Search

When a one-of-a-kind, highly qualified employee is needed, a search is an approach to be considered. After obtaining a thorough position description and person specifications, a search firm might charge an up-front fee to undertake a search, not by advertising but by calling or writing individuals presumed to have the required qualifications. The targeted individuals are not usually seeking employment, but the searchers hope to interest them in an opportunity. The fee is paid whether an individual is hired or not. Letters to individuals in key places might begin: "Do you know anyone who would be interested . . ." Recipients can nominate themselves or suggest someone else. The fact that search firms flourish suggests that they meet the needs of some organizations. On the other hand, some managers are reluctant to pay for an unknown amount of work for an uncertain result.

Technology in Recruiting

Technology is on the threshold of making major changes in recruiting practices. One application is an on-line posting system. Instead of posting job openings on bulletin boards, they can be placed in the organization's computer and made accessible to

14

HOW TO FIND THE BEST APPLICANTS

employees by means of terminals throughout the firm. An employee with a modem at home can access the system 24 hours a day.

For more efficient recruiting through the public Job Service, a software package, The Automated Job Posting Program, can be made available to employers at no charge. This enables an employer to enter a position listing in the Job Service format. That eliminates the need for Job Service personnel to fill out a form manually and then enter it into the data base, and it speeds up referrals by enabling Job Service counselors to concentrate on the professional aspects of their placement work.

A number of organizations have established data bases including résumés of people seeking employment. Some even have or can obtain videos of applicants. Fees and requirements for access to these systems vary. A partial list is included on the following pages.

The Wonderlic Organization offers a system that permits your applicants to apply by phone. Advertising carries the phone number 1-800-PhonApp plus a designated extension number. The system is loaded with a description of your company and the job, and the caller is asked a customized set of questions. These telephone applications are downloaded and sorted when it is convenient. For information call 1-800-PhonApp Extension 54321.

For both organizational and legal reasons it is important to keep track of applications in process, and software is available for this. One such system is offered by Intellectual Property Management, Inc., 14 Point Drive, Somers Point, NJ 08244.

29 RECRUITING DATA BASES

PUBLIC ACCESS DATA BASES

ADNET. Employers can advertise on-line to PRODIGY subscribers or access résumé data base. (317) 579-6922.

Career Placement Registry. Résumé bank accessible through DIALOG data base. (800) 368-3093.

15

HOW TO HIRE WINNERS — LEGALLY

Connexion. International résumé bank available through CompuServe network. (800) 338-3282.

Employers' Job Net. Electronic bulletin board. (609) 683-9191.

Exec—U—Trak. Résumé bank of Health Care Financial Management Association. (708) 531-9600 x 301.

HRIN. (Human Resources Information Network). (800) 421-8884. Databases; Military in Transition; Résumés on Computer; College Recruitment; Minority Graduate; Job Description.

HRM*NET. Human resource positions wanted and available. (703) 548-3440.

Job Bank USA. Pre-qualified résumés. (800) 296-1USA.

Job Market Inc. Job and candidate listings. (801) 484-3808.

JOBTRAK. Sends employers' job listings to colleges. (213) 474-3377.

Military Outplacement. Military and civilian employees leaving armed forces. (703) 614-5332.

Militran. (Military in Transition). (215) 687-3900.

National Career Network. Computer Search International, 630 Churchman's Road, Bldg. 3, Suite 204, Newark, DE 19702.

Printers' Résumé Network. Curtis Publishing Co., 1000 Waterway Blvd., Indianapolis, IN 46202.

Skill Search. (800) 252-5665.

Texas Savings and Loan League. 408 W. 114th St., Austin, TX 78701.

EMPLOYMENT AGENCY DATA BASES

American Association of Finance and Accounting. Ryan & Miller Associates, 5757 Wilshire Blvd., Suite 447., Los Angeles, CA 90056.

HOW TO FIND THE BEST APPLICANTS

First Interview. 5500 Interstate North Parkway, Suite 425, Atlanta, GA 30328.

Insurance National Search. Kinsale-KPJ Consilium, 68 West Main St., Oyster Bay, NY 11771.

National Insurance Recruiters Association. Shiloh Careers, P.O. Box 831, Brentwood, TN 37024-0831.

(Many local employment agencies are members of data bases.)

UNIVERSITY DATA BASES

Access/Networking in the Public Interest. Sarah Morgan Taylor, 96 Mt. Auburn St., Cambridge, MA 02140.

College Recruitment Data Base. Executive Telecom System, Inc., 9585 Valparaiso Court, Indianapolis, IN 46268.

KiNexus. Employer listings and student resumes. (800) 828-0422.

Graduating Engineers Employment Registry. Career Technologies Corp., 138 Old River Rd., Andover, MA 01810.

JOBSource. Computerized Employment Systems, Inc., 418 S. Howes, Suite D, Fort Collins, CO 80521.

Pronet (Stanford University). University Pronet, Bowman Alumni House, Stanford University, Stanford, CA 94305.

SEARCH FIRM DATA BASES

Bank Executives Network. 300 South High Street, West Chester, PA 19382

CORS. Sales Department, 1 Pierce Place, Suite 300 East, Itaska, IL 60143

Korn/Ferry Intl. 600 Montgomery St., 31st Floor, San Francisco, CA 94111.

HOW TO HIRE WINNERS — LEGALLY

Computer applications within a company's employment office may be as important as finding applicants, and software is available for purchase. Tracking applicants from receiving a résumé to acceptance of an offer is an obvious application. Computer data can be used for government reports and generating a variety for standard letters. Given appropriate data entry, a computer system can provide information to show:

- value of different sources of applicants
- number of applicants screened per hire
- length of time to fill each type of job
- differences among departments in recruiting and hiring

There will be many hardware and software developments after this book is printed. Making the most of technology in recruiting will require keeping in touch with these developments and continually canvassing users to match their needs with available systems.

Affirmative Action

Most employers know that it is illegal to discriminate on the basis of sex, race, religion, age, and physical handicaps. Less understood is the need for affirmative action in seeking out applicants from the protected classes. Many employers develop affirmative action plans for humanitarian reasons and perhaps to decrease the possibility of lawsuits.

Since 1965, affirmative action plans including goals and timetables have been *required* for companies with 50 or more employees and more than $50,000 annually in government contracts. More recent laws require affirmative action plans for the disabled and Viet Nam veterans. Each branch office of firms with multiple locations must have its own plan.

What does affirmative action mean in practice? It begins with the information required in government reports, including numbers of majority and protected groups in each job category. When the numbers of members of the protected groups are less than would be expected from the numbers in the relevant applicant pool (local for low-skill jobs; national for some professions), the organization is expected to take steps to recruit more of the protected groups. This means not merely advertising in general publications but recruiting through organizations of women and

HOW TO FIND THE BEST APPLICANTS

minorities and their specialized publications. For example, an intensive effort by Xerox in the 1960's involved parking a large trailer in the inner city and conducting employment interviews on the spot. Fisher-Price Toys operated special buses from an inner- city location to its suburban plant. Details on compliance with government regulations on discrimination and affirmative action are beyond the scope of this chapter, but guidelines are available free from local or area offices of the Equal Employment Opportunity Commission and from the Office of Federal Contract Compliance Program (OFCCP) in Washington. Many private publications also explain the guidelines.

REFINEMENTS IN RECRUITING

Job descriptions and person specifications are foundations for any recruiting effort, but there are considerations that go beyond those basics. Set forth below are some questions to consider.

1. How closely will the new hire be supervised? By what management style?
2. Do the ethical standards of the organization match those of the applicant?
3. How will the applicant fit into the existing work group?
4. Are there advancement opportunities commensurate with the applicant's expectations and abilities?
5. Can the applicant and his/her family reasonably expect to have their social, educational, spiritual, and recreational needs met in the community?
6. For management applicants, does their style fit with practices and expectations in the organization?

We know one intelligent, hard-working, and sensitive man who failed as assistant to a company president because the president's domineering style smothered the assistant to the point of adverse effects on mental health. One young, single engineer quit a satisfying job in a remote location because no social life was available. On the other hand, another company in an equally remote location was able to recruit an engineer on the basis of opportunities for hunting. A young woman failed in a management position because she was not tough enough to take control of entrenched and resistant subordinates.

In a broader sense the culture of an organization is important to consider in recruiting employees who fit. Japanese-owned factories in the United States have made extensive efforts to hire

HOW TO HIRE WINNERS — LEGALLY

employees who will be comfortable and effective under Japanese management. For example, the Suburu/Isuzu plant in Indiana identified dimensions to consider in applicants. These included team cooperation, problem solution, oral communication, work standards, ability to learn, and work tempo. Because characteristics on those dimensions are not readily assessed on a traditional employment interview, the company devised a four-step, 25-hour selection process including group exercises.

General Motors ignored the issue of recruiting workers who fit the culture when it established a new plant to build the Vega, and the result was so disastrous that the model was abandoned. Apparently learning a lesson, General Motors recruited workers for the Saturn project much more thoughtfully.

LEGAL ISSUES IN RECRUITING

Compliance with regulations on discrimination and affirmative action has been discussed previously, but there are additional legal considerations in recruiting.

When a recruiter calls former employers for information, many of them reduce the possibility of lawsuits by disclosing only position and dates of employment. It is possible to have the applicant sign a release authorizing references to give any and all information, and there is no reason for a recruiter to omit this step. Courts have generally upheld the validity of this consent form when there is no unusual problem, but that is not necessarily the case if defamation is involved. Thus the recruiter can mention or send a copy of the release, but cannot promise an informant absolute freedom from liability.

"Negligent hiring" is an issue that has recently caused serious problems and financial losses for some companies. When an employee commits a crime affecting another employee, customer, or visitor, the employer can be held liable if the employee's tendency to commit such a crime should have been discovered through interviewing or background checks. For example, a security guard company was held liable for a guard's rape of an employee because the hiring process failed to find a local police record on the applicant. Liability of an employer has also been established in cases of theft and assault by a recruit who was not investigated sufficiently.

HOW TO FIND THE BEST APPLICANTS

An employer need not conduct criminal background checks on all applicants. The extent of need for checking depends on opportunity for committing a crime. Questions involve access to keys, money, valuables, drugs, explosives, weapons, children, hospital patients, etc. Liability for negligent hiring can be minimized if the background checking is consistent with the exposure of the new hire to repeat previous criminal or antisocial behavior.

Legal Issues are explained in more detail in Chapter 8.

HIRING COSTS

The cost of advertising may be the only money paid outside the organization to hire a new employee. It is important, however, to consider all the hidden costs. Set forth below is one company's analysis of the cost of hiring an office worker.

1. *Preliminary Administration* (documenting the vacancy, getting approvals, preparing requisitions). 3 hours @ $30. $90
2. *Preparing and Sending Advertisement to Local Paper.* 1 hour @ $20. $20
3. *Week-End Ad in Local Paper.* $400
4. *Screening 20 Applicants.* 10 hours @ $20. $200
5. *Testing 13 Applicants.* 10 hours @ $20. $200
6. *3 Interviews With Hiring Supervisor.* 1 1/2 hours @ $40. $60
7. *One Medical Examination* @ $100. $100
8. *Reference Checks Before and After Some Interviews.* 4 hours @ $20. $80

Total= $1,150

The foregoing figures are in 1994 dollars, including the cost of employee benefits. Numbers of applicants and cost of advertising vary considerably. Credit checks and security clearances by outside firms would increase the cost considerably while eliminating testing and medical examination would lower costs.

A 1990 survey by the Employment Management Association found that the average direct cost of hiring a clerk was $2,785, but the actual cost of getting a clerk up to speed was $6,000 when orientation, training, and supervision were included.

21

HOW TO HIRE WINNERS — LEGALLY

The cost of hiring a professional started at around $10,000, and some hiring costs for professionals and managers went up to $100,000. Where the money goes is illustrated by the following illustration. One *New York Times* ad for a chief industrial engineer yielded 125 résumés. Ten were selected for further study and telephone screening. Expenses were paid for four applicants to visit the upstate plant; three were tested by an outside psychologist, and one was hired.

Hiring can be costly, but the cost of a mistake includes not only the costs discussed above but also the salary, supervision, and administrative costs accumulated before the discharge decision is made. It pays to select carefully.

Keeping Up With Recruiting Practices

People who spend important parts of their professional time recruiting can benefit from regularly reading *Recruitment Today,* 245 Fischer Ave. B-2, Costa Mesa, CA 92626 and *Recruiting Magazine,* 470 Boston Post Road, Weston, MA 02193. Articles on recruiting are also found in several general human resource periodicals.

References

Fine, S.A., and Wiley, W.W. *An Introduction to Functional Job Analysis.* Kalamazoo, W. E. Upjohn Institute for Employment Research, 1977.

Position Analysis Questionnaire. PAQ Services, 1315 Sunset Lane, West Lafayette, IN 47906.

chapter 2

HOW TO DESIGN SELECTIVE AND LEGAL APPLICATION FORMS

Application blanks serve three major purposes:

1. Preliminary screening of applications.

2. Guiding and supplementing the employment interview.

3. Standing on their own as primary selection devices.

The Screening Application Blank

Each purpose determines the content of the application blank. A blank designed for preliminary screening is useful in dealing with walk-ins when their numbers substantially exceed the number of job openings. Allowing applicants to complete an application form is better for public relations than the rebuff "we're not hiring." And there may be an outside chance that a walk-in might have a needed skill. An example of a one-page blank for preliminary screening is presented in this chapter, but it is labeled only "Application for Employment." It contains the essentials of:

(1) identifying information;
(2) main occupation of the applicant;
(3) recent employment; and
(4) space for any qualifications the applicant wants to high light.

HOW TO HIRE WINNERS — LEGALLY

If a company has a standing interest in programmers or tool-makers, a receptionist can be alerted to hold applicants with those qualifications for interviews. Otherwise, the form can be filed under an occupational heading, and the applicant can be informed that he/she will be called when there is a suitable opening. This blank is not burdensome for the applicant. It amply serves the purposes of preliminary screening, but more information is needed when the application blank has an important place in selection.

APPLICATION FOR SALES POSITION

Name _____ Date _____

Address _____

City _____ State _____ Zip code _____

Telephone ( ) _____

Main Occupation _____

EMPLOYMENT EXPERIENCE

Starting with your present or most recent job, list your last three jobs.

1. Company: _____
   Duties: _____
   Salary: _____
   Reason for leaving: _____
2. Company: _____
   Duties: _____
   Salary: _____
   Reason for leaving: _____
3. Company: _____
   Duties: _____
   Salary: _____
   Reason for leaving: _____
Type of work you prefer: _____

_____

State any other comments about your qualifications:

_____
_____
_____
_____

HOW TO DESIGN SELECTIVE AND LEGAL APPLICATION FORMS

The Comprehensive Application Blank

An application blank designed to make a major contribution to selection will provide more space for a description of job duties. In addition to asking why the applicant left, it can also provide opportunity to mention other reasons for leaving. Often applicants will state that they left for higher income, while a request for other reasons may reveal the more important reason, such as a fight with the boss. Asking why the applicant *accepted* a job may reveal something about motivation and goals. Additional information about the applicant may be provided by questions about aspects of previous jobs liked and disliked. A complete employment history is desirable, and this implies providing enough spaces to list all jobs.

Listing part-time jobs may reveal useful information. For some applicants it may be important to ask specific questions to elicit more information about experience in management, sales, scientific research, etc. This brings up a question about how many different application blanks a company should have. A small firm probably will want to compromise with a single blank, but large firms are likely to have three or more different blanks, perhaps one for office and production workers, a second blank for sales applicants, and a third for research scientists.

Most application blanks request information about education. Blanks for managers and scientists need space for graduate studies, seminars and workshops, and professional publications. Subjects liked and disliked in school and college can be useful. Occasionally extracurricular activities will be more significant than courses and grades. Applicants who work part of their way through college may have gained something and lost something.

Information about managerial and professional applicants can be obtained from answers to questions about their successful and unsuccessful experiences, their estimate of their relevant assets and liabilities, and their statements about career goals. An example of an application blank for sales applicants is presented in this chapter. Many of the items can be used or adapted for management and other professional applicants.

25

HOW TO HIRE WINNERS — LEGALLY

Illegal Questions

Age: Because it is illegal to discriminate against persons more than 40 years old, application blanks commonly omit any question about age or date of birth. However, a business recruiting young workers might ask applicants if they are over 18, to determine if a work permit is needed.

Name: Questions about name changes can reveal prohibited information about marital status or ethnicity, but the following question is legal: "Is any information about name changes or variations needed to check your work record? If so, explain."

Arrests: Because minorities are arrested more often, it is illegal to ask a general question about arrests. A question about convictions may be legal, however, because of the possibility of theft, embezzlement, negligent hiring, etc. However, it is prudent to add the statement: "A conviction is not necessarily a bar to employment."

Address: It is legal to ask about place of residence and how long the applicant has been a resident of the state or city, but it is illegal to ask about birthplace or the birthplace of parents or spouse.

Citizenship: An appropriate legal question is "Do you have the legal right to live and work in the United States?" Most other questions about citizenship, such as naturalization, are illegal.

Language: It is not legal to ask about an applicant's native language, but it is legal to ask about competency in languages other than English.

Relatives: The only legal questions about relatives are those relating to employment with this company. However, a legal question on the last page of the "Model Application for Sales Position" invites applicants to mention anything about family that they consider job relevant, such as having a father who is a successful salesman. This same question also opens the door for information about school and leisure experiences. The introductory phrase "employment qualifications" probably makes the question legal, although there never can be guarantees about court decisions.

26

HOW TO DESIGN SELECTIVE AND LEGAL APPLICATION FORMS

Military: General questions about military service are illegal, but it is legal to ask if the applicant wants to report any military training or experience that might be useful on the job.

Hobbies: General questions about hobbies are not job relevant, but it is legal and appropriate to invite the applicant to list any hobbies that might contribute to job qualifications. A response might include a machine shop in the garage or programming a home computer.

Organizations: A general question about organizations might illegally reveal religion or race, but it is legal to invite the applicant to list any organizations that relate to job qualifications. Responses might mention organizations of accountants, engineers, managers, technical writers, etc.

Holidays: Questions about availability for work on weekends can yield answers that reveal membership in religious groups in which work on certain days is forbidden. The government's position is that most businesses should make accommodations in scheduling when religious belief prevents an employee from working on certain days. Rejecting an applicant because of unavailability for work on certain days is legal only in the case of business necessity, as in the case of a small business with no flexibility in scheduling.

Dates: It is legal to request dates of employment, because they relate directly to qualifying experience. Listing dates of high school attendance, however, usually reveals age and is thus illegal. Schools and colleges attended can be asked without calling for dates.

Physical: It is illegal to ask questions about height, weight, disabilities, previous illness and treatment, previous absences, or workers' compensation. In the interview, however, an applicant may be given a written or oral job description identifying "essential functions" and asked if he or she can perform them without accommodation. Inquires designed to promote affirmative action for certain veteran and disabled groups are legal, but these questions can be left to the interview without complicating application forms designed for a general population. (See Chapter 8.)

Verification: It is common and appropriate for an application blank to conclude with a place to sign a statement that any

HOW TO HIRE WINNERS — LEGALLY

false or misleading information may result in discharge. A statement authorizing investigation of any statement in the application also provides some legal protection for the employer in checking references.

MODEL APPLICATION FOR SALES POSITION

Name: Date:
Address:
Position (s) in which you are interested
EMPLOYMENT. List all jobs, beginning with most recent.

Company: Dates:

What did you like best?
What did you like least?
Why did you accept that position instead of others you might have accepted at the time?

What was the main reason you left (or are considering leaving)?

What other reasons contributed to your leaving?

Income: Start   Finish

Company: Dates:

What did you like best?
What did you like least?
Why did you accept that position instead of others you might have accepted at the time?

What was the main reason you left (or are considering leaving)?

What other reasons contributed to your leaving?

Income: Start   Finish

HOW TO DESIGN SELECTIVE AND LEGAL APPLICATION FORMS

MODEL APPLICATION FOR SALES POSITION
(continued)

Company: Dates:

What did you like best?
What did you like least?
Why did you accept that position instead of others you might
have accepted at the time?

What was the main reason you left (or are considering leaving)?

What other reasons contributed to your leaving?

Income: Start   Finish

Company: Dates:

What did you like best?
What did you like least?
Why did you accept that position instead of others you might
have accepted at the time?

What was the main reason you left (or are considering leaving)?

What other reasons contributed to your leaving?

Income: Start   Finish

Company: Dates:

What did you like best?
What did you like least?
Why did you accept that position instead of others you might
have accepted at the time?

What was the main reason you left (or are considering leaving)?

What other reasons contributed to your leaving?

Income: Start   Finish

HOW TO HIRE WINNERS — LEGALLY

MODEL APPLICATION FOR SALES POSITION
(continued)

Company: Dates:

What did you like best?
What did you like least?
Why did you accept that position instead of others you might
have accepted at the time?

What was the main reason you left (or are considering leaving)?

What other reasons contributed to your leaving?

Income: Start   Finish

Please write any appropriate statements about any part-time
employment not covered above.

If your employment has included sales experience, please
describe one of your successes as a sales representative.

Please describe a sales experience that was less successful
and explain how you would now do it differently.

30

HOW TO DESIGN SELECTIVE AND LEGAL APPLICATION FORMS

MODEL APPLICATION FOR SALES POSITION
(continued)

What is most important to you in a job?

What brought about your making this application?

How would you analyze your assets and liabilities for this position?

EDUCATION
How many different school systems did you attend up through the 12th grade?
_____Comment:
Name of high school(s)_____
City_____
Major course of study_____
Rank in class_____
Please list all institutions attended after high school, in order of attendance:

Institution	Major	Class Rank	Dates	Degree

HOW TO HIRE WINNERS — LEGALLY

MODEL APPLICATION FOR SALES POSITION
(continued)

Subjects liked (college or high school)

Subjects disliked

Please add any explanation that might help us understand your educational development.

Please describe any extracurricular activities or experiences that have relevance for this job application.

Many factors may have contributed to the development of your employment qualifications. Please set forth below your analysis of these influences from any contributing source, including parents, brothers and sisters, spouse, other family members, community, school, voluntary and leisure activities.

Please describe your occupational goals or plans. You might consider time frames of one year, 10 years, and your career peak.

Are you legally authorized to work in the United States?_____yes _____no

Have you ever been convicted of a felony?_____yes _____no (Conviction of a felony is not necessarily a disqualification for employment.)

32

HOW TO DESIGN SELECTIVE AND LEGAL APPLICATION FORMS

MODEL APPLICATION FOR SALES POSITION
(continued)

I understand that statements in this application are subject to investigation and that any false statement may be sufficient cause for withdrawal of a job offer or dismissal from employment. I hereby release respondents to investigation from any liability due to releasing information about me, subject to provisions of applicable state and federal laws.

I understand that employment at (name of company) is on an at-will basis, and that my employment may be terminated with or without cause at any time, except when such termination is subject to state or federal laws.

I recognize that any offer of employment is conditioned on satisfactory results of a post-offer medical or psychological examination, results of any skill tests that may be administered, and results of drug testing if required.

Signed_____
Date_____

Government contractors are required to take affirmative action to hire disabled veterans, Viet Nam era veterans, and individuals with physical or mental handicaps. A special section may be added to the application form along the following lines.
FOR DISABLED VETERANS, VIETNAM ERA VETERANS, AND INDIVIDUALS WITH PHYSICAL OR MENTAL DISABILITIES

Government regulations require affirmative action for persons listed above. If you are a disabled veteran, a Vietnam era veteran, or a person with a physical or mental disability, you are *invited* to **VOLUNTEER** the following information, which will be kept confidential. If you are offered employment, this information will contribute to consideration of proper placement and any accommodations that may be necessary. Failure to provide this information will not adversely affect any consideration you may receive for employment or advancement if you are hired. If you desire, check the appropriate category(ies) and sign below.

___Disabled Person ___Disabled Veteran ___Vietnam Era Veteran

Signed_____

HOW TO HIRE WINNERS — LEGALLY

To Develop Or Purchase: Small companies may find it practical to purchase application forms. Some stationery stores carry them, and others are advertised by mail. There is no guarantee, however, that they are legal. The company is always liable for legality. Most application blanks designed before 1972 are illegal, and many designed after that date have not kept up with changes in laws, which have continued through 1990. It is also significant to note that some state laws differ from federal law.

It is always important to have application blanks that fit the applicant population and elicit the desired information. Of course the interview can bring out information that is not set forth on an application, but occasional discrepancy is significant. Sometimes information on the application form will eliminate the applicant before an interview is scheduled.

Compliance Information: The foregoing section discusses regulations designed to prevent discrimination in employment. An apparent contradiction lies in the regulations of the Office of Federal Contract Compliance Programs, which require records relating to affirmative action programs for women, minorities, handicapped, and Viet Nam era veterans. Such records include sex, race, physical handicap, and veteran status of all applicants, hired or not. Some state laws also require such records.

How can an employer keep discriminatory information off the application blank while collecting affirmative action data? One way is to have a data sheet separate from the application form. A heading on the compliance data sheet can state the reason for requesting the information, how it will be used, and that listing the information is voluntary.

Protection for employers requires that the compliance data sheet be separated from the application form before the application is processed and maintained in a separate file, to be available for compliance reviews. This information is necessary to determine if a protected class is adversely affected in hiring.

It is important for any business to determine the regulations to which it is subject and to set up compliance procedures

A collection of sample employment applications is available from SHRM, Attention: Accounting, 606 North Washington Street, Alexandria, VA 22314. The price is $15 for members of the Society For Human Resource Management and $25 for others.

HOW TO DESIGN SELECTIVE AND LEGAL APPLICATION FORMS

Résumés: Professional applicants commonly present résumés. Although it is tempting to accept the résumé as a substitute for an application form, it is important to remember that a resume is an applicant's advertising piece, with no more completeness or validity than an advertisement for breakfast food. In addition to the information commonly found in résumés, application blanks can provide information about reasons for leaving jobs, income, job aspects liked and disliked, career goals, etc.

When an applicant with a résumé offers too much resistance to completing an application form, a recruiter can choose to sacrifice comprehensiveness for public relations, but it is always desirable to obtain comprehensive information the employer wants instead of settling for only the information the applicant chooses to offer. When the applicant is local, it may be satisfactory to obtain comprehensive information in an interview. In recruiting from long distance, however, a comprehensive application form can be an important basis for a decision to pay transportation for a visit.

35

chapter 3

HOW TO GET THE MOST FROM APPLICATION FORMS & RÉSUMÉS

Every aspect of a completed application form or résumé can be a basis for interpretation in regard to job qualifications. It is important, however, to consider each interpretation as an hypothesis or clue, to be supported or contradicted by each subsequent piece of evidence.

General Impressions

Neatness, spelling, grammar, and organization tell something about a job applicant, but it is important to evaluate them in relation to the job. A copywriter can be expected to demonstrate near-perfect spelling and grammar, while those qualities are unimportant in a materials handler. In past years at least half of the résumés coming to my attention contained errors of spelling or grammar. Such errors are much less common since counselors and résumé services have been used more by job applicants.

Name

"Joseph P. Smith" suggests conventionality, while "Joe Smith" indicates the kind of earthy informality often found in production workers.,"J. Pierrepont Smith, III" suggests aspirations for distinction, and there may be family issues to explore.

HOW TO HIRE WINNERS — LEGALLY

Address

An applicant's address commonly offers clues to income and social class. Although it is illegal to discriminate on the basis of race, it is relevant to determine if the applicant's lifestyle is consistent with the income provided by the job.

Employment

Ideally, an applicant will present work experience consistent with job requirements. Failure to do so is often a basis for quick rejection. Descriptions of job duties can be inflated, and a recruiter may wish to make notes for clarification in a subsequent interview.

Frequency of job changes is relevant to the applicant's stability. For high turnover jobs, as in the case of food service workers, stability might not be expected. It is not uncommon for young professionals to change jobs two or three times in the first five years out of college and then settle down. Typical patterns in the occupation are important to consider. Reasons for changing jobs are also important to consider. Is there a consistent pattern of advancement, horizontal movement, or downgrading of job status? In the present era of company downsizing many applicants will claim that their jobs were eliminated. That may be the main reason more often than not, but it is important in an employment interview to explore the possibility of other reasons for termination.

Occupational likes and dislikes of applicants are likely to be repeated in their next jobs. Relationships with supervisors and peers are important, but they usually need to be explored in the interview.

Education

Most current applicants will report high school graduation, but it is important to note the type of school. Standards vary considerably, and some students are barely literate after graduation, while those taking college preparatory studies or advanced placement examinations may be brilliant. A bright student may be needed for computer programming, while the same student would be quickly bored with assembly work or cashiering.

38

HOW TO GET THE MOST FROM APPLICATION FORMS & RÉSUMÉS

High school graduation represents a critical decision time for young people. For responsible jobs it is desirable to select a person who has made realistic plans and pursued them consistently, although a 40-year-old applicant who has been a late bloomer may be qualified if the recent employment is satisfactory.

A realistic and appropriate selection of post high school education is also desirable. One recent applicant studied cosmetology but never worked at it. Instead, she took art courses, and had transferred to data processing studies at the time of her application. About half of college students change majors before graduation, but the more insightful ones remain in curricula consistent with their abilities, as in transferring from electrical engineering to computer science.

Colleges differ substantially in selectivity and in academic demands. Many honors students at open enrollment colleges could not be admitted to Ivy League institutions. Employment specialists are well advised to find out the standards of the colleges where they recruit. Information on SAT scores and selection ratios is available in several reference publications

Students who pay a substantial part of their college expenses are commonly considered more responsible than those who don't, but they may have sacrificed opportunities for leadership and developing social skills. It is important to interpret any information of this kind in relation to job requirements.

Personal Information

Although legal restrictions prohibit questions about personal information, leisure activities, and organizations, applicants often volunteer useful information. In sales work and in some other occupations, married people are more stable and successful than unmarried employees. Divorced people commonly require a year to make a comfortable adjustment.

Involvement in some organizations suggests some social interests and skills, but too many organizations (more than four) raises a question about priorities and commitment to a job. The type of leisure and extracurricular activities provides clues about energy, intellectuality, teamwork, and leadership. There are no positive implications for a person who does nothing after his work but watch television. Factory workers and foremen often hunt

HOW TO HIRE WINNERS — LEGALLY

and fish. Programming a home computer may develop skills that can be applied on the job, and it requires some intelligence. Teamwork and leadership are indicated by participation in school sports and adult organizations.

Consistency

Any gaps in dates may indicate jail, hospitalization, or jobs the applicant wants to conceal. It is important to make sure that the entire period of the applicant's background is accounted for.

Following are résumés and excerpts, with suggested interpretations. The résumé of Gary E. Schwartz was submitted in response to an advertisement for a collection manager in a small distribution firm employing 20 people.

Mr. Schwartz was invited for interviewing and testing mainly on the basis of the collection aspect of his employment as a branch manager for a financial services company. That represented a specific qualification for the advertised job. It would have been easier for the recruiter to make that connection if the work experience had been placed ahead of education. The Career Objective did not sharply target this job, however, and it is more wordy than necessary.

A closer examination of the résumé shows that the applicant has spelled "personnel" correctly in one place and incorrectly in two other places. He has also misused the work "accredit." We can infer that he is not highly sensitive to the written word but this is not a knock-out factor for a collection job.

We don't know what he did in his first year out of high school, but that omission is not necessarily significant. His enlistment in the military suggests that he did not have career plans at the time, but his military experience may have aroused his interest in financial transactions. He apparently took business courses while he was in military service, and that suggests both a career direction and ambition. His report of his high school achievement suggests college level ability, but his ambition apparently has not carried him as far as the pursuit of a college degree.

It is not clear how he came to be employed in the leather business, but the financial service experience relevant for the job opening is more recent and substantial.

40

HOW TO GET THE MOST FROM APPLICATION FORMS & RÉSUMÉS

Examples of Résumé Analysis

GARY E. SCHWARTZ
23 Beatrice Lane
Maytown, MI, 40792
(812) 987-4415

CAREER OBJECTIVE: A responsible position in mid-level management utilizing a strong background in communication skills and dealing with people including upper management, employees, and the general public.

EDUCATION: FINANCIAL SERVICES TRAINING PROGRAM — 1981-86   Extensive training in collection and lending practices. ECOA Regulations, management development, and marketing techniques.

U. OF MASS., WESTOVER AFB, MA — 1972-73 courses included essentials of business, principles of management, accounting, psychology.

USAF LEADERSHIP PREPARATION — 1974-75 Training included college accredit courses in personel management and   communication techniques together with military leadership.

HARPER VALLEY HIGH SCHOOL — graduated 1970, top 3rd of class — majored in Business Administration

EXPERIENCE:

1981-1987   BRANCH MANAGER — Acme Financial Services. Responsible for entire operation of a loan branch including lending, collecting, personnel, expense-control, and advertising.

1979-1900   PRODUCTION SUPERVISOR   Samter Belt Company, Mentor, NY. Supervisor in charge of the finishing of leather, purchasing, and inventory control.

1976-1979   COLOR TECHNICIAN — Morton Leathers, Alma, NY Mixed pigments and resins to match vinyl to leathers under different lighting.

1972-76   DISBURSEMENT ACCOUNTING SPECIALIST — U.S. Air Force. NCO in charge of collection of fines, forfeitures, and overpayments. I also handled personel with pay problems or questions on their entitlements I was also the NCO in charge of the conversation from the manual pay system to the computer pay system at _____AFB.

REFERENCES: References will be provided upon request.

41

HOW TO HIRE WINNERS — LEGALLY

The net impression of the recruiter is that the résumé of Mr. Schwartz warrants consideration of him for the collector job. The applicant does not look like a world-beater, but the level of his recent employment is consistent with the pay and responsibilities of the advertised job.

Mr. Schwartz was hired and increased collections beyond expectations in his two years on the job. Noticing that inside salespersons in the company had higher earnings, he asked for a transfer, and has been successful in sales. Of course the decision to hire was based on interview and test evidence consistent with impressions from the résumé.

The next résumé, of George Black, is that of an applicant for a job as plant manager of a fairly new and rapidly growing facility for manufacturing a novel plastic product requiring the development of new kinds of tooling and processing systems. Having grown to a work force of about 100, the facility has been managed by an entrepreneur who is not an expert in either manufacturing or the relevant technology. The new hire will be the first professional manager. The entrepreneur, a Harvard MBA, is demanding in regard to the efforts of subordinates, and he values intelligence.

GEORGE BLACK
36 Dunton Rd.
Norton, MA, 15147

PERSONAL   35 years old, 6'1", 185 lbs. Married, 1 child
                  Excellent health

EMPLOYMENT HISTORY

1975 to
Present   HARRISON MACHINE AND FOUNDRY
                  COMPANY
Duties: Manufacturer of diverse products for many
                  industries — machinery, mechanical and
                  electrical components, plus contract research and
                  engineering. Annual sales $1 billion.

                  Research Manager — Chemical Research and
                  Development. Manage department of 65 chemists,
                  engineers, and technicians.

Position: Initiation, research and development of new
                  products and processes that can be commercial-
                  ized. Design of manufacturing plants based on
                  these developments. Chemical consulting service
                  to other company units.

HOW TO GET THE MOST FROM APPLICATION FORMS & RÉSUMÉS

ACCOMPLISHMENTS OF DEPARTMENT UNDER MY LEADERSHIP

New Products and Processes

1. Completed development of a sheet material, made from waste tobacco, for use in cigarette industry. Patent protection is broad, thus permitting the company to exploit the development through licensing and royalty arrangements. My department is designing a plant for a licensee.

2. Developed a novel, ultra-thin glass paper and processes for making it. Product now being made and sold for specialty electrical insulation uses.

3. Developed a novel sheet material for use as a separator in silver batteries. This separator results in increased battery capacity and cycling life.

4. Developed a continuous flow, frothing mixer for use in making foam rubber, marshmallow and mayonnaise.

5. Developed a process and designed a plant for producing bread by a continuous process, rather than the traditional batch process. The first plant has now been in commercial operation for two years.

1970 to 1975	HARRISON MACHINE AND FOUNDRY COMPANY
Position:	Senior Chemical Engineer. During this period I was given increasing responsibility, culminating in sole responsibility for the execution of the sealing sheet project, the principal project of the laboratory at that time.
1968 to 1970	PIONEER CHEMICAL COMPANY
	Shift supervisor, power plant maintenance engineer, acid area plant investigations engineer, and finally research chemist.

EDUCATION

Midwest State University, Ch. E. with honors 1966
Syracuse University - graduate studies in chemistry 1970-71.
Alexander Hamilton Institute, business administration, 1972. Studies in higher mathematics — hobby
Tau Beta Pi, Sigma Tau, Pi Mu Epsilon, Sigma Tau Award

PATENTS

Author or coauthor of five patents or applications.
Hold main patents on the tobacco sheet process and the glass paper process.

43

HOW TO HIRE WINNERS — LEGALLY

PROFESSIONAL SOCIETY ACTIVITIES

Company alternate representative to the Industrial Research Institute, Association of Research Directors Society of the Chemical Industry ,Chemists Club, American Chemical Society, American Institute of Chemical Engineers, Society of the Plastics Industry

REFERENCES

(Applicant listed three executives of his company and a college vice president who is a consultant to his company.)

In Mr. Black's résumé we get an initial impression that it is soundly organized, with no errors in spelling or grammar. He chooses to highlight his stature, marital status, and health. These are not the most relevant job qualifications, but they can be interpreted favorably.

For a high level job, a way to begin examining an application blank or résumé is to take a chronological view, to understand how the applicant's life and career have developed. In this case we find that he graduated from a state university with honors in chemical engineering. This implies professional-level intelligence and an education that is relevant for the job. He apparently continued with chemistry studies after he earned his degree, and the implications of this are less positive, because he neither earned an advanced degree nor furthered his career.

The variety in his first professional job suggests that it was a management training program. In the interview we will want to learn why he left, but it is very common for a young professional to leave an initial job after a year or two or three, before he or she learns that the distant green pastures are no better than where he is currently employed.

He believably describes increasing responsibility in his next job as a senior chemical engineer, and he must have been evaluated favorably to be promoted to research manager.

The extent of the description of his accomplishments is more than usual, and it reflects very favorably on him. There is some question if he has offered more then the necessary detail, and we will want to see if he pursues details too much in the interview. He is evidently proud of his accomplishments, and he may be self-centered. We will want to inquire how much the accomplishments were due to his technical contributions, to his good fortune in

HOW TO GET THE MOST FROM APPLICATION FORMS & RÉSUMÉS

having productive subordinates, or to his leadership. His claim of having patents suggests that he made some individual technical contributions and that he may be creative. His present job seems like a reasonable stepping stone for our job opening. His work has involved pilot manufacturing operations, but it has had more emphasis on research and development. We need to find out if he will be comfortable leaving research and concentrating on manufacturing.

His reported involvement in professional societies is much greater than usual. This may mean paying dues without learning much or contributing much. If he has a high level of involvement we might wonder about his priorities in neglecting the job for which he is paid. The résumé gives a clear impression that he is intelligent enough, with adequate technical foundation, and relevant experience. Additional questions to explore in the interview are:

1. How self-centered and egotistical is he?
2. What is his principal role as a leader—one of inspiration, creative example, decision making, or laissez-faire?
3. What qualities enabled him to advance so fast in responsibility—creativity, problem solving, likeability, ruthless aggressiveness, organizing ability, etc.?

After further interviewing and psychological testing Mr. Black was hired, and he presided successfully over a four-fold expansion of the plant. His style was more authoritarian than participative, but this was compatible with the expectations of the founder/entrepreneur and with the type of labor that was recruited.

Weighted Application Blanks

Most completed application blanks are evaluated clinically, by examining each one individually, as in the preceding examples. Under certain conditions, however, application items can be given numerical weights that make them useful selection tools. Biographical data in application blanks has successfully predicted tenure or performance of salesmen, cab drivers, YMCA secretaries, aircraft pilots, supervisors, and zinc miners. Conditions necessary for development of weighted application blanks are listed below.

45

HOW TO HIRE WINNERS — LEGALLY

1. Large numbers of people are employed in the same type of job.
2. There is a valid quantitative measure of job success. Weighted application blanks have been proven most effective in predicting tenure. They have not been effective in predicting quantity, quality, or supervisor's ratings.
3. There are substantial variations in the measure of job success. If there is low turnover, there is not enough variation to develop item weights.
4. Substantial numbers, at least 50, can be identified as clearly successful, with an equal number unsuccessful.
5. Clerical time is available for tabulation.
6. An employee or consultant is available to perform the not-too-difficult statistical analysis.

In the past, application blank items relating to age, marital status, number of children, height, and weight have contributed to the validity of a weighted application blank. Those items can no longer be included legally. However, consideration can be given to items relating to length of employment in previous jobs, changes in career direction, length of time at residence, school achievement, school curricula, subjects liked and disliked, career goals, earnings, self-descriptors, etc.

A generalist human resources manager who wishes to consider developing a weighted application blank can employ a consultant, probably an industrial psychologist. Descriptions of the technique, however, can be found in the following references.

Welch, J., Stone, C.H., and Paterson, D.G. *How to Develop A Weighted Application Blank*. Research and Technical Report 11, Industrial Relations Center, University of Minnesota.

England, G.W. *Development and Use of Weighted Application Blanks*. Dubuque, Iowa: Wm. C. Brown Co. 1961.

Impostors

John Wilson was an applicant for vice president of marketing in a firm employing 1,000 people. A major qualifying job was listed in his application form as seven years as a district manager in a sales organization. For his most recent two years of employment, however, he listed himself as a consultant. Such a listing is always suspect because it cannot easily be checked. In

46

HOW TO GET THE MOST FROM APPLICATION FORMS & RÉSUMÉS

the Education section of his application blank he indicated: "B.S. Comm, 1972, Ohio State University, Law LLB 1974, Ohio Bar Association."

In the first place, a law degree usually requires three years after the bachelor's degree. In the second place, lawyers tend to list only "LLB." The "Law" is redundant. In the third place, a law degree was irrelevant for the marketing job. In fact his application showed that he worked as a salesman the next year after earning his law degree.

English skills in his résumé were at a professional level, but his oral English in the interview contained some imperfections not usually found in lawyers. Subsequent testing also revealed a lower level of intelligence than his claimed education would suggest. A call to Ohio State did not find his name listed among law graduates, and his name was not on a list of members of the Ohio Bar Association. He apparently trapped himself by claiming qualifications with which he was not familiar enough. The basis for suspecting his credentials started with the questionable dates on his application.

Following is a portion of another résumé that raised suspicions on several grounds. Harold Hill was an applicant for the position of controller in a scientific firm employing 300 people. He impressed the president so much that the usual employment procedures were almost bypassed.

RÉSUMÉ OF	30 Elm Street, Mosport, NH
HAROLD HILL	Telephone (207) 716-6759

EDUCATION AND AFFILIATION

Wayne University, Detroit, MI June 1963, B Sc Engineering Physics Additional credits, Sorbonne, Paris, France, "Sustained Ultra-High Pressures" Past Fellow Of the Royal Astronomical Society, Foreign Member of the Royal Meteorological Society and member of the American Meteorological Society. Founder of Evaluation Services, Inc., and the Rocket Society of Washington, D.C. Member, Operations Research Society of America, Operational Research Society - London.

EMPLOYMENT

Aug. 1986 to Feb. 1988	Manson Machine Co.	Portland, Maine
Controller and	Acme Specialty Machinery	Nashua, N.H.
Dir. Corp. Plans		
Sep 1982 to July 1986	Astro Dynamics, Inc.	Weston, Mass.
(Marketing/Sales)	Em Gee, Inc.	Milton, NY
	Data Acquisition	

47

HOW TO HIRE WINNERS — LEGALLY

Nov. 1975 to Sep 1982 Multiple Mfrs. Rep (Self Empld)	Electrical Components Engineering Services A/D Systems, PC and Magnetic Components	Utica, NY
Oct. 1967 to Nov. 1975 (Consultant)	Campbell & Neville Electronic Publications	New York, NY
	Design Services Co. Engineering Services	Newark, NJ
	Superior Electrical Ind. Electrical Products	Hollywood, Fla.
	Broadway Electronics, Inc. Communications	Red Bank, NJ
May 1966 to Oct. 1967 (Research Associate)	Smithsonian Institution Astrophysics	Washington, DC
(Senior Meteorologist)	Intercontinental Airlines	New York, NY
Jan. 1960 to Apr. 1966 (Engineer/Supervisor)	Sanford Instrument Co. General Motors	New York, NY Detroit, Mich.

Half of the second page of the résumé contained a description of his duties under the heading "Management." The other half described duties under a "Marketing/Sales" heading. A third page described duties under an "Engineering" heading. Under a heading "Publications and Patents" he named five papers, all in private company publications and one patent applied for.

There is so much to question in this résumé that it is difficult to know where to start. The first section catches the reader's eye because of the unusual connection with foreign societies and technical references to meteorology, astronomy, and operations research. Few normal people could deal effectively with such a wide span of specialized technologies, but a paranoid schizophrenic could imagine them.

Also unusual is the applicant's listing more than one apparently full-time job in each of the last two time periods, and these jobs were in different cities. The same condition was shown in the 1966-67 and 1960-66 time periods. In the two periods when he was self-employed he could have represented or consulted with multiple firms, but, as mentioned earlier, employment as a consultant is often listed by people who were unemployed or minimally employed. It is not subject to checking. His listed publications are also not subject to easy checking because they are in-house, and his patent is only "applied for."

48

HOW TO GET THE MOST FROM APPLICATION FORMS & RÉSUMÉS

The time period 1960-66 is highly suspect. He claims he earned a four-year degree in a rigorous curriculum while employed in both Detroit and New York in jobs that are normally full time.

Identifying items in this résumé have been changed, but it represents a real person. The items raising suspicions include:

1. Inconsistent dates.
2. Grandiose affiliations, including foreign ones.
3. Employment in engineering, marketing, and controller work (where did he learn enough accounting to be a controller?)
4. Self-employment that is difficult to check.
5. Publications that are not accessible to the public.

This applicant was referred to a psychologist, whose report described a con man, with terrific self-presentation but lack of the creativity, organizing ability, and stability implied by his résumé and required in the job of controller. The company president found it difficult to believe the psychologist, but he took the report seriously enough to reject the applicant. The applicant returned to the psychologist for feedback on his test results. In response to the psychologist's candid statements, Mr. Hill readily admitted that much of his résumé was fabricated. The psychologist suggested that he could be a very effective salesman and have high earnings without pretense and falsification of his background, but Mr. Hill insisted on maintaining his facade, and he was confident that he could be hired in some high level job by the next firm.

chapter 4

HOW TO INTERVIEW EFFICIENTLY AND LEGALLY

General Principles and Considerations

In a few instances an employment interview may be the only basis for a job offer. More often it supplements and complements an application form or résumé. Purposes of the interview include:

1. Amplifying and clarifying information from application forms and résumés.
2. Eliciting new information.
3. Supporting or contradicting information from tests and reference checking.
4. Evaluating the presentability of the applicant.
5. Providing the applicant with information about the job.
6. Developing impressions about motivation, interpersonal skills, and other personality characteristics.
7. Contributing to the organization's public relations by leaving the applicant with a positive feeling regardless of the hiring decision.

Why Interviews Have Been Poor Predictors Of Job Performance

Employment interviews, by themselves, have had minimal success in predicting how well a person will perform after being hired. Following are some reasons for this.

1. Many interviewers have not been trained.
2. The artificial interview situation does not necessarily represent an applicant's typical behavior.
3. Interviewers are not always consistent in their approach.
4. First impressions may have too much influence.

HOW TO HIRE WINNERS — LEGALLY

5. Grooming and verbal fluency may have a "halo effect" that causes an overestimate of the applicant. A "negative halo effect" may also occur.
6. Many interviewers have biases against women, minorities, fat people, short people.
7. Interviewers may fail to elicit critical information.
8. Interviewers may be unduly influenced by applicants seen before and after a particular interview.

This chapter undertakes to provide a basis for improving the usefulness of employment interviews.

Before the Interview

Every organization wants to hire somebody sometime. That requires making the organization seem like an attractive place to live and work. It begins with the neighborhood, which human resource people may not be able to control. Next is the outside of the building, which also may be difficult to change. But inside the building it is important to give attention to the things that will make the place look attractive to applicants.

That does not necessarily require expensive furnishings; in fact designer furnishings can be overdone if they are not consistent with salaries and working conditions. But any walk-in office can be free from litter, with places to sit and hang outerwear. Anyone walking in deserves a courteous greeting and an honest response about the time to wait for an interview. That means realistic scheduling by interviewers. In the event of unavoidable delays applicants deserve to be kept informed. Offering a beverage or mint is a nice gesture, but this is not to suggest that such an offer is necessary or appropriate for all offices.

Receptionists can be selected and trained to convey the impression (we hope honestly) that they like the company. They can maintain a professional atmosphere, with a minimum of gossip or distraction. Employees can think of applicants as guests in their home and act accordingly.

In times of labor surplus many applicants will be only too happy to accept offers of employment regardless of their impression of the company, but they may not be the best qualified. When labor is in short supply and when certain qualifications are in short supply, the initial impression of applicants can be critical.

HOW TO INTERVIEW EFFICIENTLY AND LEGALLY

It is not uncommon for applicants to walk away after they have seen the building or to walk out before waiting for an interview.

When multiple interviewers are involved it is important to make sure that they will be available and to schedule them realistically. Sending the applicant a copy of the schedule is also sound practice. Applicants will feel more comfortable if a host is assigned to provide a plant tour and guide them to their appointments. When only a few jobs are open, "knockout" questions can eliminate many applicants. Some topics are listed below:

1. hours of work
2. transportation
3. licenses or certifications
4. income required
5. special skills like keyboard speed or tolerances in machining

When applications or résumés are mailed in, these kinds of questions can be asked on the telephone, saving time for both applicant and employer. A screening interview with walk-in applicants can sometimes be conducted standing up, although the value of saving time needs to be weighed against the effect on public relations. Whenever an applicant shows unexpected promise, the interview can be continued more thoroughly. In most instances applicants who are screened out can be given to understand that they will be called and interviewed more thoroughly when there is a job opening for which they qualify.

Preparing for the Selection Interview

The privacy required for an effective interview can be obtained in a private office or conference room, with interruptions only for emergencies. Distractions interfere with the rapport and may cause neglect of some information.

Comfortable chairs, preferably of equal quality for interviewer and interviewee, are desirable. One of my favorite interviewers moves from behind his desk to join the applicant in identical lounge chairs.

Some interviewers are reluctant to take notes, but studies have shown that this is not distracting if it is done considerately. Thus a writing surface is needed.

53

HOW TO HIRE WINNERS — LEGALLY

Audiotaping or videotaping may be used in some circumstances such as a research project. However, it is important to remember that reviewing a one-hour interview on tape requires a second hour of professional time. Notes suffice in most instances.

Interviews are most useful when the interviewer collects and studies all available information beforehand, including application form, test scores, reference information, and comments of a receptionist or colleague. This information is a basis for identifying points to be elaborated, gaps to fill in, items to be confirmed or contradicted, a suitable starting point for questioning.

Having a thorough understanding of the job requirements is essential. In a large organization, the interviewer will have a job specification to study. Reviewing person specifications is equally important. The interviewer should find out not only what the boss is looking for but also the characteristics associated with the success or failure of previous job holders.

Scheduling enough time for the interview is important. That includes not only time for questioning and listening but also some time for describing the job and responding to questions from the applicant. Studies have shown that interviewers talk, on the average, two-thirds of the time in a typical employment interview. Experts recommend just the opposite distribution of time. Interviewers can't learn about an applicant while they are talking themselves.

Illegal Questions

Chapter 2 explains questions that are illegal to include on application forms. The same questions are also illegal to ask in employment interviews. They include questions about age, birthplace, citizenship, native language, arrests, military discharge, hobbies, organizations, race, sex, religion, and physical impairments.

However, it is not illegal for an interviewer to listen if an applicant volunteers information on these points. Most of them are not job-relevant anyway, but if an applicant mentions being hospitalized, for example, it is legal to inquire about the reason and present physical condition.

54

HOW TO INTERVIEW EFFICIENTLY AND LEGALLY

A clear understanding of legal and illegal questions is important before beginning an interview. Legal issues are reviewed and discussed in more detail in Chapter 8.

Breaking the Ice

Putting the applicant at ease and establishing a relationship are essential for gaining the maximum benefit from an employment interview. This is accomplished through the amenities of ordinary social life, such as shaking hands and inviting the applicant to sit. A relaxed but interested attitude on the part of the interviewer is desirable. Some interviewers develop rapport by mentioning a topic of general interest, like the latest ball game. If carried too far, however, this takes the interview in the direction of a social chat. A more relevant ice breaker is preliminary discussion of some item in the application form, such as common acquaintance with some previous employer or shared occupational or educational experiences.

At times it will be useful to ask if the applicant has any preliminary questions or anything he/she wants to mention at the outset. Sometimes the applicant will relax better if questions about parking, the location of the bathroom, or length of the interview are cleared up promptly. What applicants say in response to an initial opening may reveal factors relevant for selection if questions relate to vacations and benefits on the one hand or responsibilities on the other hand.

Information about the Company

In any employment procedure it is important to distinguish between getting information and giving information, although a smooth interview does not necessarily separate these functions sharply. A common approach is to use five minutes near the beginning of the interview to mention key features of the job opening to make sure of the applicant's genuine interest in this position. More details can be added later if the selection aspects of the interview are proceeding favorably. In some situations, details of the job duties will be discussed by a department head after an employment specialist has interviewed with more of a focus on the applicant. In a tight labor market it may be necessary to "sell" the applicant on the job, but an applicant who is oversold will soon leave.

HOW TO HIRE WINNERS — LEGALLY

In larger organizations it is a common and useful practice to present the applicant with a brochure listing important features about the company. Such a brochure can have both a selling function and an informative one. It cannot be assumed, however, that every applicant will read and understand all the written information. It is always desirable to cover key points in an interview. These include a concise statement of job duties, hours of work, income possibilities, and reporting relationships. Other items likely to be less important but of legitimate interest to the applicant include: advancement prospects, benefits, projections of company growth, stability of employment, bonuses and incentives, financial aid for transfers, tuition aid, eating facilities, parking, and recreational facilities. The amount of detail can be influenced by time available and by the extent to which the applicant makes a favorable impression. It is the interviewer's responsibility to make the job seem as desirable as possible within limits of honesty.

Principles of Questioning

The most important principle in employment interviewing is to use open-ended questions, beginning with words like Why, What, How, and To What Extent. Questions that permit a Yes or No answer let the applicant off the hook too easily. It may be all right to use them to clear up a question of fact, like "Do you have a driver's license?" but an objective in the employment interview is to obtain full explanations, and open-ended questions are required to accomplish that.

There are responses like "I did mechanical engineering" that fail to tell what the interviewer would like to know. It is always all right to ask "Would you explain that more?" or "Can you tell me more about that?" Responses to those questions may provide opportunities for additional follow-up questions on the same topic, like "What kind of customers did you visit?" or "What type of projects did you work on and what was your particular contribution?"

Inferences about personality characteristics can be made from responses to questions like "How did you feel about that? What did your boss say about that? What was your relationship with peers? Supervisors? Subordinates?

56

HOW TO INTERVIEW EFFICIENTLY AND LEGALLY

Although it is illegal to query applicants about their personal lives, relevant information often comes out voluntarily, as in the statement "That was right after my divorce" or "When I came out of the hospital..." It is legal and appropriate to follow up with requests for further explanation of any topic that the applicant has voluntarily introduced.

Some applicants get carried away in recalling traumatic events, even to the point of crying. Normal interpersonal courtesies apply in such instances, and the interviewer can refrain from questioning until the applicant's poise is regained. It is prudent not to take notes at such times, but a strategy is to make necessary notes at some other point in the interview. A note does not have to be made exactly at the time an applicant mentions a sensitive point, especially if it has legal implications.

Many interviews can proceed in a straightforward approach, perhaps proceeding chronologically through an applicant's background. However, a rigid pattern of questioning discourages the applicant from enriching answers. A smoother interview is achieved when the interview follows any leads that turn up, to develop some theme to its fullest extent. For example, if an applicant says something like "I had always wanted to try selling," it might be appropriate to ask when and how that interest developed and then return to the original framework after the point is developed enough to be a basis for interpretation.

Any employment interview is somewhat stressful for the applicant, if not for the interviewer. Some applicants become angry or otherwise emotional during an employment interview. Strong emotions interfere with the objective gathering of information and impressions. If they arise, one strategy is to shift to a less stressful topic. Another strategy is to bring the interview to a close as soon as it can be done smoothly and perhaps schedule for an additional interview at another time if there is still a possibility that the applicant could be selected.

Some interviewers have deliberately introduced stress into interviews with questions like "Why haven't you advanced faster in your career?" Such an approach will reveal something about the applicant's reaction to a certain kind of stress, but it won't tell much about a person's ability to perform most jobs in industry. A stress interview may be appropriate for selecting spies for the CIA, and in fact it has been used for that purpose, but it is counterproductive in selecting candidates for most jobs.

HOW TO HIRE WINNERS — LEGALLY

Pauses after an applicant's response are an effective way of eliciting more complete answers, particularly if the interviewer looks expectant. Pauses introduce some stress, but not usually to an excessive extent.

Sensitive interviewers try to adjust their language for most effective communication with particular applicants. Professional language is appropriate for professional applicants, but it might fail to communicate with some applicants for positions in materials handling. Specialized terms like "byte" or "HVAC" are appropriate only when it is clear that the applicant is supposed to understand them. Interviewers elicit more from applicants when they maintain an attitude of interest and encouragement, but objectivity is important. Any indication of disapproval may cause an applicant to limit responses.

Employment Experience

An employment interview appropriately begins with some attempt to break the ice, and some description of the job opening. After that, a decision is needed regarding where to begin the substance of the selection aspects. Starting with a discussion of the applicant's work experience is the most expected, and it is unequivocally relevant. For an applicant with significant experience, it is reasonable to begin with the current or most recent job. That is likely to be the most significant qualification. After that there is another choice of whether to work backwards through the employment history or perhaps to jump back to a first or early job and move forward. The latter approach often makes it easier to follow the characteristics and influences in a person's career development. In the case of fairly new graduates of high school or college the questioning can begin with a discussion of education.

If the applicant is employed, a question about reasons for considering a change may bring out useful information. In regard to any job, the interviewer needs information about:

1. Thorough description of duties and responsibilities.
2. Income.
3. Achievements.
4. Difficulties or failures.
5. Aspects liked and disliked.
6. Advancement, if any, in responsibilities and income.
7. Reasons for taking that job in the first place.

HOW TO INTERVIEW EFFICIENTLY AND LEGALLY

When the author asked one retail salesperson to describe the duties of her job she said, "I sell." There was a long pause to permit her to continue, but she never did. The tentative conclusion from this exchange was that the applicant was an overly laconic person with a minimum of flexibility. That impression was confirmed when she failed to respond any more fully to further questions.

A contrasting interpretation can be made when an applicant spends 15 minutes describing the minute details of a simple job, including the idiosyncrasies of supervisors and who said what at every point in job tasks.

In evaluating information about income and advancement it is important to consider the situation. When an organization is downsizing advancement is not expected, while in a rapidly expanding organization some people may advance faster than their abilities would justify. College graduates are expected to advance faster than employees without a college background. In certain technical and secretarial jobs no advancement is expected or available.

The aspects of the job that are liked and disliked provide clues about the applicant's satisfaction in the next job. Liking broad responsibility can be interpreted favorably in a management candidate, but the candidate may not necessarily be sincere in saying what the interviewer would like to hear. A liking for detail work is appropriate for the work of an accounting clerk but not for a salesperson or manager. Some applicants will say that they like the technical problem solving in jobs like engineering or work in a model shop. That can be interpreted favorably in regard to consideration for similar jobs. Likes and dislikes relating to supervisors and associates provide clues about relationships in a new job. People who have difficulties with authority are likely to have the same kind of experience in the next job. Appropriate questions deal with preferences for stability versus variety, independence, responsibility for other people, travel, or overtime. Has the person been frustrated because of his/her inadequacies or because of verifiable external conditions like downsizing of the company? Has the person taken initiative to improve his or her job status?

Reasons for taking a job are at least as significant as reasons for leaving it. People with minimal education are likely to accept the first job offer, often in their neighborhoods. Obtaining a job

HOW TO HIRE WINNERS — LEGALLY

through a relative is common, but it does not reflect any planning on the part of the applicant. Taking a job for the specific duties or advancement opportunities can be interpreted favorably, if that is realistic in the situation. It is not uncommon for naive applicants to say that they took a job for the advancement opportunities when no such opportunities could be realistically expected. Taking a job in a school cafeteria in order to be with one's children after school is reasonable for a person who places family considerations foremost, but that does not reflect any particular career interests. One applicant said that he became a school teacher because of the summer vacations, not a favorable indication of success in the sales job for which he was applying.

Reasons for leaving a job are commonly included in an application blank. The interview can amplify those reasons, and a relevant question is "What other reasons were there?" An applicant will often state a commonly acceptable reason like "higher pay" when a more important reason might be a fight with the boss or too much responsibility.

Education

It is always desirable to know the schools the applicant attended, major subjects, scholastic standing, subjects liked and disliked, and subjects in which highest and lowest grades were earned. The amount of mathematics completed in high school is significant for jobs with mathematical components like accounting, estimating, drafting, and cashiering.

In regard to scholastic achievement, it is important to note that high school class rank is commonly assigned on the basis of whatever subjects the student has taken, whether college preparatory, business, art, or other. A student electing a more difficult curriculum may be penalized in terms of rank. Furthermore, there is a wide variation among high schools in academic competitiveness. Graduates of some high schools are barely literate, while a high percentage of students from other schools are accepted at Ivy League colleges. Scores on standardized tests like the SAT and ACT provide a check on claims of high school achievement, but accurate reporting of any academic information cannot be depended upon.

Students who have changed schools several times may be handicapped academically. The social effects may help them to

HOW TO INTERVIEW EFFICIENTLY AND LEGALLY

make initial acquaintances easily but at the expense of depth in relationships.

When some applicants are questioned about subjects liked and disliked they respond that it depended on the teacher more than on the subject. This type of response suggests a person whose effectiveness and satisfaction may depend less on job duties than on a "happy family" atmosphere in the organization. Such a person would be less effective in independent job assignments.

For applicants with some college experience it is appropriate to inquire about the reasons for choosing a particular college and curriculum. The student who chooses engineering, accounting, or some other clearly occupationally oriented curriculum and follows through to employment can be regarded as planful and responsible. But such students are more exceptional than common. To fill the ranks of business and industry it is necessary to hire some people who are less consistent. Half of college students change majors. An interviewer appropriately looks for evidence that the individual has stabilized on a career track that is suitable in regard to abilities and interests even if there has been some previous exploration and re-direction.

Ideally, the choice of a curriculum precedes the choice of a college. To study engineering it is necessary to apply to a college that offers it. Not all applicants make choices that are realistic in this regard. The selectivity of colleges is readily available in several reference works, such as *Lovejoy's College Guide*. Acceptance at a selective college is a sound indication of academic ability. Many students choose open enrollment public colleges for financial reasons. Enrollment at such a college doesn't tell much about scholastic ability, but graduation from a rigorous curriculum does. At many state colleges less than 50 percent of the enrollees graduate, but the ones who do are probably competent academically. Most applicants are honest in reporting facts about their work experience and education, but there is an occasional liar or impostor. For applicants who are college graduates **it is strongly recommended that a transcript be obtained.** Employment is not easy to check, but any applicant can ask to have a transcript sent to a prospective employer. An employer's telephone call to the college registrar will usually verify that the applicant graduated from a particular curriculum in a particular year, but that is all.

61

HOW TO HIRE WINNERS — LEGALLY

Extracurricular Activities

There is no doubt that out-of-class activities in high school and college contribute to development of skills and attitudes that affect job performance, but the relevance might be difficult to prove if questioning along these lines is challenged by a female or minority applicant. Information about extracurricular activities is often volunteered. If so, it can be interpreted. A legal question might identify person specifications for a job, such as organizing ability or creativity and then ask, "Have you had any extracurricular experiences that contributed to the development of (the named characteristics)?" A general question about all extracurricular activities is legally questionable.

There is a widespread belief that aggressive participation in team sports contributes to qualifications for management and sales work. Election to captain may suggest leadership capacity, but football tackles and basketball centers make the team primarily because of their size, although experience in teamwork may be useful in business. Participation in individual sports like running and tennis indicates physical energy, but it would be difficult to draw general conclusions about personality. The long hours of practice required to earn a letter in some varsity sports may actually detract from broader social and intellectual development. There may even be some negative influence from illegal recruiting and encouraging or condoning of dirty play. Success in debating would be a useful background for a lawyer or a salesperson. Fraternity or sorority membership suggests some degree of socialization and social acceptability.

Personality and Motivation

"What characteristics of yours have contributed to your successes and difficulties in any of your previous jobs?" is a question that may elicit some useful information. A related question is: "What are the most important personal characteristics that you can bring to this job?" Another possible question is: "Is there any aspect of this job that might be difficult for you?" Although questions like these invite the applicant to mention only favorable characteristics, my experience indicates that applicants mention characteristics that have some support in other evidence. A few applicants even admit that they are lazy or careless.

It is appropriate to ask applicants why they want this job and why he or she might prefer it over a present or previous job. A

HOW TO INTERVIEW EFFICIENTLY AND LEGALLY

question about hopes for job advancement can be followed by a question about what the applicant thinks he or she would need to do to qualify for that advancement. Young people don't always think about that. Evaluation of responses needs to take into account the experience of the applicant. Applicants with ten years of business experience can be expected to be more realistic than recent college graduates. Questions about relationships with supervisors and the kind of people an applicant likes to work with are legal and sometimes useful.

A broad general question can be made legal if it is related to the job, as in the following:

"Many factors can contribute to the development of employment qualifications. Is there anything you would like to tell us about your development of qualifications for this job through any of your experiences in family, school, employment, or leisure activities?" Such a question doesn't necessarily yield any useful information, but occasionally an applicant will say: "My father was a salesman and I became a salesman because I admired him" or "My parents wanted me to be a doctor, but I couldn't get into medical school, and I'm hoping this job will start me on a career where I can be successful" or "I like to work with my hands, but my wife wants me to get into white collar work." It is illegal to ask a direct, general question about family, but asking applicants to elaborate on a point they have brought up can often yield useful information without raising legal questions.

Control of the Interview

It is the responsibility of the interviewer to control the interview. In most cases this involves encouraging the applicant to offer more complete explanations. Some interviewees, however, offer excessive detail about unimportant matters. Others try to take control. I recall one applicant who leaned forward, said "let me tell you about myself, and went on for 15 minutes before taking a breath. Exercising smooth control, both encouraging and limiting, is more art than science, but practice helps, and it helps to keep in mind the points to cover and the selection criteria. There is no point in continuing beyond the point that the impression is unequivocally is negative, although it is important to terminate the interview tactfully.

HOW TO HIRE WINNERS — LEGALLY

It is the responsibility of the interviewer to bring the interview to a close, perhaps with "Thank you. I appreciate your cooperation, but I don't have any more questions." The interviewer has an obligation to indicate what will happen next, including when the applicant can expect a decision about employment or if additional investigation or interviewing is required. No applicant should be left hanging indefinitely.

The Patterned Interview

The preceding pages have described the type of selection interview that is appropriate for interviewing candidates of different types with as much depth as possible in a flexible manner. Comparison of different candidates is enhanced when the interviewer uses a consistent approach while flexibly following the applicant's leads when appropriate.

Greater consistency can be attained at the expense of depth and flexibility by using a patterned approach. A patterned interview can be used appropriately when it is necessary to interview large numbers of applicants for jobs with a minimum of complexity, like short-contact salespersons, warehouse workers, and temporary construction laborers. As in other selection situations, it is preferable to have an application form at hand during the interview. Knockout questions can be introduced early. Care needs to be given to the development of questions before interviewing is done. It is easier to follow the pattern if these questions are written out and placed where the interviewer can glance at them. Some questions suitable for a patterned interview are listed below.

- How did you learn about this job?
- Why are you interested in it?
- What are your qualifications for this job?
- What do you regard as your main occupation?
- Why did you leave (or are considering leaving) your last job?
- Do you have any disabilities that would prevent you from performing all the duties of this job?
- Would you have any problems with the hours and working conditions of this job?
- Do you have transportation that will permit regular attendance?
- What is the highest level of education you have completed?
- What are your long-range career plans?

HOW TO INTERVIEW EFFICIENTLY AND LEGALLY

- What jobs have you had before your present (or most recent) job?
- How long were you employed in each job?
- Why did you leave each job?
- Please describe any periods of unemployment you have had.

The foregoing questions are not intended to represent one complete or typical patterned interview. It is important for each patterned interview to include knockout and qualifying questions and as many deepening questions as time and interest permit.

Multiple Interviewers

In a small organization an applicant may appropriately have only one interview, with the boss. In many organizations an employment specialist might conduct the first interview, touching on general educational and occupational background. This interview might be followed by an interview with a department head, covering a more detailed description of the job and exploration of specialized qualifications by discussing projects and equipment worked on, types of customers or publications, and examination of examples of the applicant's work. As many as eight people have interviewed applicants in some companies, but that probably is excessive. When more than three interviewers are used scheduling problems commonly result in uneven evaluation of different applicants for the same job. A strategy for broad exposure of an applicant is to invite prospective coworkers to lunch with the applicant.

The Interview Panel

Instead of arranging successive individual interviews, it is possible to have an applicant interviewed by two or more people at the same time. This has the advantages of saving the applicant's time and providing all interviewers with a sample of the applicant's behavior to observe. There are important disadvantages, however. One is that the applicant may feel more threatened, resulting in less openness in responding to questions. Another is that personality dynamics among the interviewers may affect all parties in ways that confuse prediction of the applicant's future behavior on the job. Problems include disagreements among panel members and monopolizing the time by one or more panelists.

65

HOW TO HIRE WINNERS — LEGALLY

Coordinating and Training Interviewers

Whenever more than one interviewer is involved, especially in a panel interview situation, it is important to agree beforehand on what each will do and to agree on time frames for each subject. Some give-and-take can be permitted; one interviewer may think of a clarifying question that the first questioner did not think of. But adherence to some general plan and schedule is important.

Coordination in evaluating interview interpretations is also important. This can be achieved by developing a framework or set of criteria beforehand and sharing evaluations afterward. This can be enhanced by independent completion of an interview evaluation form, which the several interviewers might meet to discuss. An example of an evaluation form or guideline is represented in Figure 1 at the end of this chapter.

Interviewing effectively requires skills that can be learned through training. Large organizations may be able to hire interviewers who have studied psychology and interviewing techniques in college. If new training is required for some employees, many metropolitan universities offer evening courses in interviewing and related topics. Some of these courses include role playing sessions in which students practice with a videotape, which can be critiqued afterward.

HOW TO INTERVIEW EFFICIENTLY AND LEGALLY

Figure 1.

CHARACTERISTICS	RATING A - E	COMMENTS

General Impressions

Appearance
Poise
Body language
Vocabulary
Grammar
Organization of ideas

Employment History

Qualifying experience
Career path
Stability
Advancement
Goals
Any problems?
Fit with job opening
Underqualified
Overqualified
Future prospects

Education

Specific qualifications
Scholastic achievement
Planning
Subjects liked; disliked
Earn school expenses?
Extracurricular: impli-
cations about energy,
teamwork, leadership,
sociability, etc.

Other Sources

Health
Leadership
Emotional stability
Relevant skills
Finances

*Family (illegal to ask
but may be volunteered)*

Early influences
Spouse
Siblings
Children

67

chapter 5

HOW TO SPOT WINNERS AND LOSERS

Transcribed Interview Segments and Interpretations

Two Secretarial Applicants

An interview with Mary Simmons began with discussion of a job in an advertising agency, from which she was laid off when the agency lost an account. Because she had little work experience, the interviewer went backward in her life, and the following dialogue ensued.

I.   When you were in high school, how did your plans for the future shape up?

A.   Ever since sophomore year, I had wanted to be a missionary. I was only 17 when I graduated, and my parents objected to it, so I thought I'd work a year and then go. So I worked as a clerk in a circulation department and entered the missionary order the following year. I was there almost four years. I left before the course was completed.

(Because the applicant volunteered this information, the interviewer could legally ask "What sort of course was that?" She explained that it was primarily religious, with some secular study about South Sea Islanders, to whom she would have been sent.)

Comment: This is an example of how revealing surprises may turn up. Neither the missionary training nor the first job had appeared on her résumé. The interviewer had the impression that the applicant had no intention to falsify her résumé but had only set forth what she thought was relevant. Subsequent dialogue indicated that her missionary commitment receded and that she was now comfortable in a more conventional secretarial role. The interview continues.

HOW TO HIRE WINNERS — LEGALLY

I.   What are you looking for in a job now?

A.   Someplace where there is room for advancement and also room for a lot of interest and nice surroundings—people who enjoy their work.

I.   Oh huh!

A.   And as I say, you're dealing with people and personalities and not just sending out bills.

I.   When you say advancement, what does advancement mean to you—Where would you want to go with your career?

A.   Oh. I don't know (laugh). I mean just a job where you can keep interested in it.

I.   Do you want to be in charge of other people in an office, or does advancement mean more pay or what?

A.   Well, maybe enough different things to do or a chance to learn something new.

Comment: The interviewer seeks to find out about her goals and values, first by asking a general question. He takes note of what she says and follows up her response about advancement. The interviewer's last question in the section is leading (a questionable practice), but it appears necessary because of the applicant's failure to make a clear response to the general question. When she is pinned down about advancement, she leaves the impression that she did not really mean advancement in the usual sense and that she may have been merely saying what she thought she was supposed to say. She finally leaves a clear impression that she prefers intrinsically interesting work and is not driven by money or power. The interviewer's "Oh huh" represents a technique for soliciting more information, and it worked here to a modest extent.

The interview eventually covered the full range of work experience and education, with consistent impressions, leading to the conclusion: "employable but limited." Some principles illustrated in these brief excerpts include:

70

HOW TO SPOT WINNERS AND LOSERS

1. Open-ended questions can produce results, sometimes surprising.
2. "Oh huh" can elicit more information.
3. A leading question can be useful as a follow-up, not as the initial introduction of a topic.
4. An applicant does not necessarily follow the direction suggested by a leading question.
5. Job-related values can be brought out in an interview.
6. Interviews don't necessarily yield useful information about job skills.

People have infinite variety. Following is an excerpt from an interview with another secretarial applicant, 30 years old and unmarried. After discussion of her main employment, the interviewer asks:

I. Will you tell me about your education?

A. Yes. Well. I loved school. Probably if I had my druthers I'd go to school the rest of my life. I enjoyed school and I was in a lot of things—student government, and I was editor of the yearbook, and my high school had a plan where if you were good in English they had a Clarion class which means that you were responsible for getting out the school newspaper and the rest of the time was entirely left to the teacher and the class— anything you wanted to do. Well, it was a fascinating class of course, and English happened to be my strong point—the class I liked most, so I had a very nice senior year. Oh, I was a class officer in my junior year, and I was in the student government for the first three years, but when I became editor of the yearbook I had to drop out of a lot of other things. Usually as far as social things went in high school I was with a crowd. Now that I think back everything we did was in a group. I think the only time I went out with a fellow all by myself was just two or three times . . .

Comment: The foregoing is only a quarter of the applicant's response, which went on about her limited social life, her lack of money for college, the expectations of her immigrant grandmother that she become a homemaker, and her change of perspective after she began working.

The interviewer didn't do anything special to elicit this uncensored outpouring, but it shows a result from an open-ended question. The applicant has revealed that she has high verbal skills, had some leadership experience, values education, and

71

HOW TO HIRE WINNERS — LEGALLY

probably is uncomfortable about being unmarried. Her rambling about personal matters suggests that she may lack objectivity and that her concern about herself may interfere with ability to distinguish relevant from irrelevant information. With this type of applicant a strategy is to allow some rambling in the beginning of an interview but to regain control at some point. In this case the interviewer cut off a long discussion of her supervisor to ask, "Can you tell me how your duties developed?" The applicant got the message and said, "Oh, yes, if I talk too much just tell me."

A response to an open-ended question that elicits more relevant information, this time about employment, is set forth below. It comes from a 50-year-old secretarial applicant who has been asked:

I. Can you tell me more about what you were doing? (on a job that has been identified by company and title)

A. Well, it was a little of everything. It is a very small place, and of course in a place like that you do just about everything that's to be done; I didn't take care of the books; they had an outside auditor. I was secretary-treasurer of the company. I also worked in the factory and on the machines as well. He used to take care of the payroll and that sort of thing, but as far as all of the office work was concerned I did that. We had a lot of foreign shipments and of course there was a lot of foreign papers to clear the shipments. Filing. I wrote all my own letters. There wasn't any dictation. They would just tell me a word here and there and I'd build it up accordingly . . . I would order all the parts for the various finished articles and check finished work. I took care of mailing. Just because it was a small place you do everything.

Comment: The applicant is confident enough to provide information without prompting. Most of it is relevant, but the organization of her ideas could be improved. She clearly had substantial responsibility but her English is imperfect, e.g., "There was a lot..."

The employment process does not always work out neatly, with time for the interviewer to prepare by reviewing an application beforehand. The following excerpt is from an interview where a consultant did not have access to a résumé or application form before beginning an interview with a young applicant for industrial sales work.

72

HOW TO SPOT WINNERS AND LOSERS

I.   I would appreciate it if you will start in and tell me the highlights of your background.

A.   Well, I'll start with high school. I took a college prep course in high school, and upon completion of that I went into the Navy. I spent three years in the Navy as a radio operator and made 2nd class petty officer. After that I went to (a two-year technical institute), taking construction technology. I took the major courses in physics and math, and then I withdrew from college because it wasn't holding my interest.

I.   After one year?

A.   After one year, and I started working for . . . Corporation as a management trainee. I worked there approximately nine months with the understanding that I would go into sales upon completion of my training period. They didn't think I was ready or they didn't have any available space for a salesman, so I wasn't able to go into the sales force. So they kept me in the laboratory in quality control, and after a couple of weeks I asked them for a raise, and they told me it was impossible to get a raise . . . so I left and went to work for . . . Originally they said they were selling teaching machines with programmed instruction, but it turned out they were just out to sell books and the teaching machine itself. They want $800 from families that can't afford it, and they play on the educational thing. They offered me a chance to go to NY to act as a management supervisor, but before I would be able to go I would have to sign out for money, you know to open the office, and I would have to buy desks and chairs and everything that went with it I would have to rent. So I would have to go in the hole, so I put my application in here.

Comment: The very open-ended opening question does not fit every applicant, but it is not unreasonable to ask a sales applicant to think on his feet. In this case the applicant is fairly systematic in touching on highlights of his education, military service, and his brief employment experience.

He is fluent, and he organizes well enough, but his brief employment in each of two jobs is not impressive. It seems probable that he is impatient. He may be immature or naive in failing to find out enough about his two employers before he was hired. His report of his schooling suggests that he is intelligent enough for industrial sales, but his career planning is open to question. He says he dropped out of college for lack of interest. Failing

73

HOW TO HIRE WINNERS — LEGALLY

grades are always a possibility in these cases. The interviewer tried to learn more about this with "After one year?" But the applicant didn't bite. The interviewer could have returned to questions about college later in the interview or asked the applicant to have a transcript sent. (As stated elsewhere in this book it is always appropriate to ask for a transcript wherever education is important. It is not particularly important in this case.)

Later in this interview the interviewer asks how the applicant came to take his first sales job after leaving college.

A. Well, I found myself in college, a lot of times—I would get on these social committees. I was social chairman of my fraternity, and I found that I was having a lot of progress and a lot of self-satisfaction by talking with people and talking them into things and talking them out of things. And then I got a job as a radio announcer in one of the local stations.

I. This was employment for pay?

A. No, not pay. It was volunteered. Just for the school. And I had a program every week... and I found it very interesting, talking to people in the advertising department, and they suggested that I might try to get into sales because I sort of had the talent for it. And I did enjoy talking to people and being with people. So I decided maybe sales was what I wanted.

Comment: Liking to talk to people is ok for a salesperson, but it is not enough. Successful sales workers also want to make money, and they purposefully make their own plans and decisions. It is not clear that this applicant is that mature, although there are some favorable implications in the reported comments of his associates at the radio station. This applicant freely volunteers information, sometimes without realizing the implications of immaturity. After this interview the applicant was tested by a psychologist, and the findings of immaturity influenced rejection by the employer.

To show how a stronger applicant responds to interview questions, the following excerpt is taken from an interview with an applicant for the position of vice president and director of client services with an advertising agency. The applicant's résumé showed a BA in journalism and philosophy with honors and an MS in advertising with honors, in addition to professional semi-

74

HOW TO SPOT WINNERS AND LOSERS

nars. He listed increasingly responsible positions in advertising, ranging in length from two to six years.

In response to questions he stated that he left most of his previous jobs because of an "opportunity to grow." He left one job because he did not have enough control, and he left another because his boss was not a risk taker. After reviewing his work experience the interviewer asks:

I.   What are the main assets you can bring to this job?

A.   People management is my strongest suit. I developed a performance appraisal process for subordinates. I clarified each person's responsibilities and had them develop short and long range career goals. All of my subordinates were eventually promoted.

I.   What are your liabilities, if any, in regard to the job duties that we have outlined?

A.   I don't think I have any. I have done all the things, and my success has been at a high level.

I.   Can you tell me more about what you expect to do in this job if you are hired?

A.   The company expects me to motivate and grow people, and I can do that. I expect to develop new business; I know how to analyze prospects and develop presentations. My presentation format focuses on the prospect. I also expect to develop the agency's visibility in the community...

Comment: This applicant presents a solid record of accomplishment (subject to verification). He supports his assertions with specific points about his performance appraisals, promotion of subordinates, and his approach to presentations. The impressions from this interview were entirely favorable, although that does not eliminate the possibility that negative information could come from tests or references. As it turned out this applicant tested very well and was hired.

An applicant for a job selling wholesale paper had experience mainly as a routeman. He did not make a particularly favorable impression in the interview, but the dialogue followed conventional patterns until the end, when the interviewer followed the

75

HOW TO HIRE WINNERS — LEGALLY

appropriate practice of leaving the door open for the applicant to add anything he felt important.

I. I'm interested in anything that reflects your experience and qualifications and how you fit with this job. Can you think of anything else important in your background that you would like to mention?

A. No, I can't think of anything—I don't think of anything more right now. There's only one thing that I would like to have someone else's opinion on. As far as this job is concerned I'd like to get somebody else's opinion—it would have to be yours or somebody that knows me. I have a feeling that as far as meeting people or anything like that, I have no trouble—I mean I enjoy—I like people. But people's first impression, I feel that it would be a handicap to me if people feel that maybe I'm too young to be out selling a particular thing. And I know that after I met the person that I could make them feel that I'm not and that I'm sincere in what I'm saying, but first indications, like maybe this particular type of job, well, you don't get—you know, you don't actually say, get to know the people. Maybe you would after you come back, but I mean, would that be a handicap to me as far as selling, any type of selling?

Comment: The applicant had not made a very favorable impression up to this point, but here he really shoots himself in the foot. His admission that he lacks confidence in presenting himself is a clean knockout. He seems to be seeking emotional support from the interviewer rather than selling himself for a sales job. His rambling discourse also indicates limited intelligence and poor organization of ideas.

How Questions Get Results

From the standpoint of interviewing technique, this illustrates what can come from the final question, "What else?" Not many applicants hang themselves but this one did.

The foregoing interview excerpts demonstrate the following points.

1. An interview can yield considerable significant information, favorable (the vice president) and unfavorable (the sales applicant who fears he makes an unfavorable impression).

HOW TO SPOT WINNERS AND LOSERS

2. Open-ended questions can yield important information.
3. Closed-ended questions yield only specific answers to specific questions.
4. A grunt can elicit more information on a topic. (Silence can also.)
5. Following an applicant's leads contributes to the smoothness of an interview.
6. Surprises may turn up in responses to open-ended questions (the missionary background of a secretarial applicant and the lack of confidence of a sales applicant).
7. When applicants talk too little or too much, the interviewer can take control.

The foregoing excerpts from real interviews do not illustrate all possible techniques and responses. Readers are encouraged to study books focusing primarily on interviewing. These books often include ideal questions and answers that are neater than real life, but readers might find ideas they can use.

Interviewers are also encouraged to record samples of their interviews for study. Video equipment is within reach financially, and audio is very inexpensive. Interviewers who don't want to expose their work to other critics can at least review tapes for themselves. Tapes reveal that most of us are not so smooth as we think, but we can all improve.

chapter 6

HOW TO TEST JOB APPLICANTS LEGALLY

The previous chapters, on application forms and interviews, deal with subjects familiar to employment specialists and human resource generalists. The appropriate and legal use of tests, however, requires specialized knowledge. This chapter discusses what human resource generalists need to know in order to obtain training in testing or to employ the services of test specialists. It is beyond the scope of this book to make the reader a test specialist.

Background

Applications of testing in job placement began with the Army Alpha test, which was used to classify soldiers in World War I. That test and its derivatives were used subsequently for selecting people for civilian jobs.

In the 1920's and 1930's the emphasis in psychological testing shifted from the general to the specific. An observer might have inferred that human beings were composed of hundreds of separate aptitudes and abilities, each of which some psychologist was busily trying to measure. Current *Mental Measurements Yearbooks* list more than 1,000 published tests, and this listing does not include tests that have gone out of print or are available only through private sources.

Personality tests and most tests that are administered individually are sold only to people with educational credentials in tests. Tests that can be purchased by business firms include tests of general intelligence (whatever that is), mechanical aptitude, clerical aptitude, manipulative ability, arithmetic, and special aptitudes for word processing, computer programming, and the like.

HOW TO HIRE WINNERS — LEGALLY

Types of Tests

Intelligence Tests

Many studies have found a relationship between scores on intelligence tests and job performance. These relationships are never strong enough to prove that the highest scorer will be the best employee, but they are strong enough to be considered as one of several factors in selection.

Research has identified bands of intelligence test scores found in different occupations. Highest scorers are found in professions like physics, chemistry, engineering, and psychology (tests are developed by psychologists). Top managers score high, technicians and some clerical workers a little below, and unskilled laborers are at the bottom. A score above the range of an occupational group can be a *negative* factor in selection because the work might not be challenging enough.

Although psychologists recognize that intelligence may be comprised of a number of abilities (they don't agree on how many), practicality has resulted in three types of items in paper-and-pencil tests of general intelligence. Examples are:

A. *Father* is to *Son* as *Mother* is to: (1) aunt (2) sister (3) daughter (4) child.

B. 2:8=8: (1) 16; (2) 64; (3) 32; (4) 96

C. □: ⬜ = ○ : (1) ⬜ (2)△ (3)○ (4)○

The word and number problems, especially, are based on the type of learning promoted in school, and in fact the highest relationships between test scores and achievement are found in school. People who have not experienced a standard and satisfactory American schooling are at such a disadvantage that these kinds of tests are unsuitable for use with them.

Tests of Special Aptitudes

Mechanical aptitude tests have been found useful in selecting apprentices, drafters, and machinists. They may require identification of tools or which way a seesaw will descend when the weights or distances from the fulcrum are unequal. The pictorial items involve cars, boats, pulleys, gears and other items

80

HOW TO TEST JOB APPLICANTS LEGALLY

common in American culture. Reading requirements are minimal, but mechanical experience contributes to higher scores. A maintenance mechanic can score higher than an engineering student.

Clerical aptitude tests require good perceptual ability in identifying, on a closely timed basis, similarities and differences between pairs of numbers and names or classifying numerical and verbal items according to specified categories.

A word processing test measures ability to interpret instructions in a manual. A computer aptitude test includes the kind of numerical and verbal items found in intelligence tests, plus a flow-charting exercise following instructions in the test.

Sales aptitude tests briefly describe selling situations, followed by multiple choice questions.

Manipulative Tests

Tests are available for measuring speed in handling small objects and large objects, using tweezers, and using tools like wrench and screwdriver.

Multiaptitude Tests

The General Aptitude Test Battery, consisting of eleven subtests, has been administered by the state employment services on behalf of employers. The 23 occupational aptitude patterns identify job applicants who qualify for all, some, or none of those occupations. Because minority applicants score lower on some of the subtests, states began a practice of race norming, that is, ranking applicants only within their ethnic groups. Referrals were made to employers without informing them of this practice. After it became public, the practice was discontinued. In 1990 the Department of Labor announced that it was planning to discontinue use of the GATB because of discrimination concerns, but a storm of protest from employers caused the Department to change its mind. In the meantime, some states decided not to use the GATB without race norming. In late 1992 the government contracted with a private firm to revise the GATB. This process will require considerable time, but employers who hire skilled labor would be well advised to check with their state employment services to find out what testing can be available to them.

81

HOW TO HIRE WINNERS — LEGALLY

Multiaptitude tests of private publishers include the Employee Aptitude Survey (EAS) and the Flanagan Aptitude Classification Tests (FACT). Norms and validity data are much less comprehensive than the data on the GATB.

Proficiency Tests

Typing tests have been widely used for a quick check on the typing speed and accuracy of clerical applicants. They are still applicable in offices where electric or electronic typewriters are used. However, the norms (standards) for typing tests do not apply to word processors. Some placement agencies have developed tests on their equipment, and they will send scores to an employer, although they have a vested interest in reporting high scores. An office manager can be on the lookout for tests that may be developed on the latest office equipment and which will not be unfair to applicants who are not currently experienced on that equipment. Schools teaching word processing usually will send reports to employers. In the absence of precise comparison standards, some useful impressions can be gained by trying out secretarial applicants on the equipment in use and making subjective observations.

Tests of spelling are available, but they are less important in an office with word processors that have built-in spelling checks. It is doubtful if there is any current need for the shorthand tests that have been used. An accounting achievement test has been developed by the American Institute of Certified Public Accountants, but its use is restricted. Tests for electricians, machinists, drafters, and electronic technicians have been developed, but it would be inappropriate to use them without a careful review of the content to determine if it is current.

Sensory Ability Tests

People who do fine assembly, accurate clerical work, and some jobs in graphic arts require good near-point vision. The Big E chart in an industrial nurse's office measures far-point vision at an optical distance of 20 feet, but it cannot be counted upon to measure near-point vision. Standard vision tests by ophthalmologists and optometrists do not necessarily measure the visual ability required in some jobs unless such a measurement is specifically requested. Where vision is a problem in job performance special devices can be obtained for administration in the employ-

82

HOW TO TEST JOB APPLICANTS LEGALLY

ment office. Two suppliers are Titmus Optical Company (804) 732-6121 and Stever Optical Company 1-800-244-9500.

When auditory acuity is a factor in selecting applicants it may be necessary to have a hearing test done by a specialist outside the plant. Seldom can such a test be done in an industrial setting. Pre-employment hearing testing is a two-edged sword. It is important for some jobs, but a test establishes a baseline for comparison if subsequent tests show a decline in hearing acuity. The employer may be liable if it can be shown that the hearing loss was caused by excessive noise in the plant.

Color perception is important for some jobs involving plastics, paint, crayons, electrical wiring, and natural fibers. About seven percent of men have some degree of color blindness, and their color vision cannot be assumed. (Color blindness is possible but rare in women.) Color perception tests can be purchased from test publishers.

Personality Testing

Personality questionnaires are used in industry by professionals who have credentials that permit them to buy the tests. Scores have occasionally shown a relationship to job success for salesmen and other occupational groups. More often, however, no relationship to job success has been shown. More validity has been shown for describing people in counseling settings, where the counselees are presumed to be motivated to reveal themselves. A job applicant, on the other hand, is motivated to present the most favorable picture, and the tendency to "fake good" is strong. Scores useful for predicting job success usually depend on the applicant's self-insight and willingness to be entirely candid. A rare exception has been when adjustments were made for the tendency to "fake good."

These questionnaires include questions like, "Have you ever crossed the street to avoid meeting somebody? Do you often feel depressed? Do you tire easily?" Most job applicants can answer in ways that make them seem well adjusted.

Projective personality tests almost eliminate the faking problem, but they create other problems. An examinee is asked to tell a story about selected pictures, to tell what ink blots look like, or to complete sentences beginning with stems like "I like . . . " or "My father . . ." Training in interpreting these tests is in the do-

83

main of clinical psychology, and not many clinical psychologists practice personnel selection. Interpretations are usually descriptions of personality, not scores. Thus they are not subject to the kind of quantitative validation implied by government regulations. Some dramatic predictions have been made from projective tests, like the report that an advertising applicant was creative and intelligent but so tense that he would unwind like a broken spring within a year. He was hired and performed very well until he cracked up in six months and went to work picking apples. However, clinical psychologists have not found ways to apply statistical validation techniques to personality descriptions in ways that find general acceptance.

Honesty Tests

Stores, banks, and other organizations concerned with theft have used polygraph testing in the past, but Congress has outlawed the use of the polygraph except in special circumstances, such as those involving public safety.

As an alternative, publishers have developed paper-and-pencil questionnaires that purport to detect potential for theft and other undesirable behaviors. Publishers claim significant validity, but critics point out that the studies have been done by the publishers themselves, without peer review. Scoring keys are proprietary and are not released to other professionals for independent research. Available studies indicate no adverse impact on minorities, but passing rates are 40 to 70 percent. Huge applicant pools are required if 30 to 60 percent of the applicants are rejected. Furthermore, the base rates of detected theft are too low for optimum statistical manipulation. No doubt many thefts go undetected. The failing rates indicate that the number of false positives probably is high. In a 1984 article Sackett et al. concluded that none of the honesty tests could be depended upon to do the job for which it is intended. However, in a 1989 article, based on accumulating evidence, the same authors concluded that honesty tests could be useful to a company with the luxury of rejecting many applicants but that these tests could not dependably predict the behavior of individuals. (Sackett, Paul, et al; *Personnel Psychology*, 42, 2, 491-529, 1989.)

Several states are considering outlawing honesty tests, and it will be important to keep abreast of legislation in this area.

HOW TO TEST JOB APPLICANTS LEGALLY

Interest Inventories

Interest inventories were originally designed to help school and college students identify occupations where their interests might bring them job satisfaction. They include statements relating to occupations like the following.

- Keep records of materials on hand and supplies received.
- Care for patients in a hospital.
- Teach sports to young adults.
- Fix a clock.
- Play a musical instrument.

Respondents are asked to indicate Like or Dislike or to choose the most liked and least liked items in a group of three. These inventories are useful in helping young people choose careers and predicting subsequent job satisfaction. They can also be used in-house in industry in helping employees plan career paths.

However, interest inventories have very limited use in hiring from the outside because they are too easy to slant. Applicants have every reason to answer the inventories in ways that are appropriate for the job. It is conceivable that scoring procedures could be developed to compensate for faking, but that has seldom been tried.

Assessment Centers

An assessment center includes standardized evaluations of a group of several assessees performing standardized exercises under the observation of trained assessors. This approach was first used for selecting German army officers, later adapted by the British army, and modified for selecting operatives of the CIA in World War II.

In industry, the original model was developed by AT&T, to identify employees qualified for promotion in management. Job analysis identified a number of qualifications, such as oral communication, planning and organizing, initiative, decisiveness, and tolerance for stress. Ways of evaluating these characteristics included paper-and-pencil intelligence tests, background information on education and employment, leaderless group activities, case analysis, and in-basket exercises derived from realistic business situations. For example, one in-basket item asked the

HOW TO HIRE WINNERS — LEGALLY

candidates to write a letter to the Public Service Commission justifying a rate increase. AT&T selected line managers for training as assessors. Other companies adapting the assessment center approach include IBM, Sears, Roebuck, J.C. Penney, Mobil, etc.

Predictions of the subsequent job success of assessees have varied, but they have been significant more often than not. Assessment center approaches have been used for selecting new hires also.

Written tests used in assessment centers have shown adverse impact, as in other situations, but this has been balanced by lack of adverse impact in the behavioral exercises. The face validity of assessment centers, with exercises based on job analysis, has resulted in few challenges. At this writing in 1992 I am not aware of any successful challenge to personnel decisions based on assessment center evaluations. Women and minorities have generally held their own in assessment centers. In early experiments difficulties were found when one woman was assessed with five men in a group. However, the addition of a second woman seemed to solve that problem.

Another benefit of assessment centers is the effect on both assessees and assessors. The exercises are learning experiences, and feedback to participants helps them understand themselves and criteria for advancement in the organization. The assessors also learn to define and evaluate characteristics required for job success.

Assessment centers for identifying promotable employees are necessarily limited to large organizations, where there is a sufficient supply of candidates and assessors, as well as the required financial resources. These procedures are expensive. Candidates and assessors may be occupied for an otherwise unproductive week, or at least several days. Developing exercises is also very expensive. Attempts have been made by consulting organizations to assess in one group candidates from different organizations that are not large enough to develop their own centers.

In selecting new hires there are cheaper ways than assessment centers. Interviews with employment specialists and line managers are usually included anyway. An assessment of one day or less by a qualified psychologist *can* yield as valid a prediction of success as an assessment center at much lower cost, although the validity of such assessments has not been documented to the

86

HOW TO TEST JOB APPLICANTS LEGALLY

same extent. They have less face validity, and they are more subject to challenges by rejected minority and female applicants.

For companies large enough to organize assessment centers it is possible to engage a consulting organization with experience in their development. The potential benefits in predictions, relative freedom from EEO challenges, and development of participants can be weighed against the substantial costs. Smaller organizations can adapt some of the job analysis aspects of assessment centers by developing their own behavioral tests, as described in the following section.

Testing with Job Samples or Simulations

If a test derived directly from job analysis is administered to a job applicant, a validation study probably is not required to comply with government requirements. Validity is established through the job analysis.

One example is a typing test. A purchasable test is usually regarded as satisfactory for ordinary secretarial jobs that involve writing letters and reports. However, a specially developed test might be needed for statistical typing.

Applicants for machine sewing can be tested on a sewing machine. Machinists can be tried out on a machine. Applicants for assembly work can be tested on a replica of the task. A test for directory assistance telephone operators presented a sample of recorded inquiries from callers and recorded the accuracy and time of responses of applicants. In developing tests for "area mechanics" in a Xerox plant psychologists met with foremen of plumbers, carpenters, and electricians to identify knowledge required in each craft, such as what tools to bring for erecting Hauserman (movable) office partitions, and then constructed multiple choice tests, which were tried out on incumbents before administration to applicants.

A job sample test for toy salesmen arranged for a candidate to press a button at a work station to hear the objections of a prospective customer, after which the candidate's response was recorded. Similarly, an interview with prospects for sales work in a bank included a description of a customer, and the interviewer made notes of the applicant's explanation of how to approach that customer. One simulation stated that a pregnant young woman came in with her husband; they explained that they were new in

HOW TO HIRE WINNERS — LEGALLY

the community, and the door was left open for the applicant to suggest the most appropriate bank services. Applicant responses were scaled according to a hierarchy of responses classified by a panel of "experts." Applicants for management can be asked how they would handle common situations like excessive absenteeism or disputes between employees.

The foregoing paragraphs suggest how simulations can be used in selecting people for many types of work. Effort is required to develop, score, and standardize work samples, but their face validity almost eliminates challenges from applicants or the government.

Legal Issues in Testing

Any employment procedure is subject to government regulations regarding discrimination. Discriminatory items have been removed from most application forms. Employment interviews have seldom been challenged, perhaps because results are not quantified and are not usually recorded.

Tests, however, have been challenged a number of times. In one case (*Griggs v. Duke Power*) an intelligence test was found not to be job related. In another, testing was not administered under standard conditions. Ratings against which tests were validated were inappropriate in other cases.

It is important for any organization using tests to be aware of the regulations and to be prepared to show the validity of any tests used. In the first place, records of applicants must be kept to determine if there is adverse impact in hiring. Minorities commonly score lower than Caucasians on many paper-and-pencil tests, resulting in adverse impact if applicants with higher scores are hired. The government's "four-fifths rule" states that the hiring ratio for any group must be at least four-fifths the ratio for the favored group. In the absence of adverse impact, an organization *might* not have to justify its employment procedures, but the courts have not been consistent enough to guarantee that. When there is adverse impact, the organization must stop testing or produce a validation study demonstrating a substantial relationship between test scores and job success. The government has specified that the statistical relationship shows legal validity if it would occur by chance not more than five times in 100. Explaining the statistical procedures is beyond the scope of this book. The purpose here is to show the obligations of an employer when-

88

HOW TO TEST JOB APPLICANTS LEGALLY

ever there is adverse impact in hiring and if it is challenged. Those conditions do not always occur when tests are used. In Chapter 8 suggestions will be offered for minimizing legal challenges in selection.

Buying Tests

Tests can be very useful in selecting employees, but their legal, and meaningful application by human resource generalists requires a commitment to understand test manuals that include terms like the following: *norms, reliability, validity, correlation, mean, standard deviation,* and *standard error of measurement.* Also required is a commitment to take responsibility for meeting the legal requirements of the government, to provide evidence of validity if testing results in adverse impact on the protected groups. Many organizations have given up testing rather than try to meet those requirements.

At the end of this chapter is a list of some test publishers. An organization accepting the risks of testing can write for a catalogue of each of several test publishers and then write or telephone for sample sets of the tests that seem to have potential for that organization's hiring problems. A decision to purchase a test can be based on answers to the following questions about information in the test manual.

• Is the test desired for use with our types of job applicants?

• Are there validity studies showing significant relationships between test scores and job success?

• Are there norms for our types of job applicants?

• Are enough people represented in the norms (more than 100)?

• Has the nature of the job or the applicant population changed since the normative data were collected?

• On the basis of our job analysis, can the test be defended as job relevant?

Publishers' claims that the test meets EEO requirements are suspect. There is such a thing as "synthetic validity," determined

89

HOW TO HIRE WINNERS — LEGALLY

by matching a new organization's job analysis with analysis of the same job in a different organization where validity of a test has been established. However, such matching is technically and practically difficult, and there is no guarantee that it will satisfy a government compliance officer. There is no such thing as "general validity." A test is valid only to a certain level of statistical significance with a specified population and compared with a specified measure of job success.

Once an organization has decided that a test is defensible and potentially useful in selection, the following administrative questions need to be answered.

• Can the security of test materials be assured with a locked file to which there is limited access?

• Who will be responsible for test administration, interpretation, and test security?

• Is there a place where testing can be done **without distraction** or interruption?

• If the test is timed, can we do that accurately? (A stop watch or photographic timer is needed.)

• Can we store completed test papers securely, apart from the personnel file?

• Will test scores be given to applicants? To managers?

Large organizations may be able to employ people with credentials to buy tests and awareness of the requirements for useful and legal testing. Smaller organizations can reduce their risks and increase the probability of benefits by employing credentialed consultants.

Specific tests have not been described in this section because of the possible distortion in selecting from hundreds. Human resource professionals who wish to review specific test possibilities are referred to *Business and Industry Testing* by Joyce and Robert Hogan, published in 1990 by Pro-ed, 8700 Shoal Creek Boulevard, Austin, TX 78758. A more comprehensive source is the *Mental Measurements Yearbook*. Current editions of this large reference work can be found in libraries. Both publications offer critical reviews of tests and addresses of publishers.

HOW TO TEST JOB APPLICANTS LEGALLY

Types of Test Publishers

Types of tests mentioned in the foregoing discussion can be purchased from publishers, which, in their test manuals, report studies of reliability and validity and describe normative populations. This information is open to the psychological profession for evaluation, and critiques are published in reference books like the *Mental Measurements Yearbooks*. These publishers assume responsibility for selling tests only to qualified users, who then have the responsibility for appropriate and legal use.

Proprietary test publishers, on the other hand, emphasize selling a service rather than selling tests. They may or may not expose their tests for professional critiques, and they commonly maintain control of the scoring keys. Completed test papers may be scored through computer systems or sent to the publisher for scoring. This control means that proprietary test publishers may share the responsibility for using a test legally. It also implies that the user needs to trust the publisher or scoring service for meaningful scoring and interpretation of scores.

SELECTED TEST PUBLISHERS

Center for Applications of Psychological Type, Inc. 2720 N.W. 6th St., Gainesville, FL 32609.
Consulting Psychologists Press. 577 College Ave., P.O. Box 60070, Palo Alto, CA 94306.
CTB/McGraw-Hill. Del Monte Research Park, 2500 Garden Rd., Monterey, CA 93904.
EDITS. P.O. Box 7234, San Diego, CA 92107.
Institute of personality and Ability Testing, P.O. Box 188 Champaign, IL 61821.
Jastak Assessmemt Systems. P.O. Box 4460, Wilmington, DE 19807.
Jist Works, Inc. 150 E. 14th St., Indianapolis, IN 46202.
Martin M. Bruce. 50 Larchwood Rd, Larchmont, NY 10538.
*London House. 1550 N. Highway, Par Ridge, IL 60068.
National Computer Systems. 10901 Bren Rd., East, Minnetonka, MN 55343.
Personnel Press. 191 Spring St., Lexington, MA 02173.
*Personnel Decisions, Inc. 2000 Plaza Seven Tower, 45 South Seventh St., Minneapolis, MN 55402.
Psychological Corp. 555 Academic Court, San Antonio, TX 78204.
*Reid Psychological Systems. 233 N. Michigan Ave., Chicago, IL Phone (312) 938-9200.

HOW TO HIRE WINNERS — LEGALLY

Research Psychologists Press. 1110 Military St., P.O. Box 984, Port Huron, MI 48061-0984.

Sheridan Psychological Services. P.O. Box 6101, Orange, CA 92667.

SRA/London House. 1550 N. Northwest Highway, Park Ridge, IL 60068.

*Stanton Corp. 5701 Executive Center Drive, Suite 300, Charlotte, NC 28229.

Stoelting Corp. 1350 S. Kostner Ave., Chicago, IL 60623.

Western Psychological Service. 12031 Wilshire, Los Angeles, CA 90025.

Wonderlic Personnel Test, Inc., 820 Frontage Rd., Northfield, IL 60093-8007.

Psychological Services, Inc. 100 W. Broadway, Suite 1100, Glendale, CA 91210.

*Proprietary

chapter 7

HOW TO AVOID NEGLIGENT HIRING

The Importance of Checking

Surveys have found that between 20 percent and 80 percent of résumés contain inflated or false information. Employers who accept at face value all the information on résumés and application blanks are exposing themselves to considerable risk. In the first place, every employer wants to hire people with integrity. In the second place, specific qualifications may be important. Thirdly, there is exposure to a charge of "negligent hiring" if an employee commits a violation that could have been predicted by an investigation.

Several people practicing as physicians have been exposed as impostors after a malpractice incident triggered an investigation. Professors have been exposed after a belated check revealed false claims of degrees. After a *Washington Post* reporter confessed to having fabricated a Pulitzer Prize winning story it was found that she did not have the master's degree or the Vassar degree with honors that she had claimed. One of my client companies hired, despite questionable psychological test results, a person with a Ph.D. in a very esoteric field. They gave him a laboratory and paid his high salary for two years before they discovered that he had not accomplished anything useful and was so disturbed that he was committed to a mental hospital. His (false) credentials were so impressive that they had not bothered to check them despite my strong recommendation.

In at least two publicized instances landlords have been sued for hiring, without prior investigation, employees who raped tenants. One of the employees was a house painter; the other a secu-

HOW TO HIRE WINNERS — LEGALLY

rity guard. Retailers have been sued for hiring employees who have assaulted customers or stolen from them.

Lay a Foundation for the Investigation

By means of the application form and the interview, it helps to get as many references as possible, not pastors and neighbors, but supervisors, professional associates, clients, customers, vendors, and the like. Insisting on a complete work history, including dates, may reveal gaps that call for explanation. That may identify more places to check.

It is prudent to have the applicant sign a form releasing information for former employers. All applicants claiming graduation from college within the last 15 years should be asked to have their transcripts sent. If this step is omitted, a phone call to most colleges will yield verification of the degree and date but nothing more. In 16 states the laws permit employees to have access to their personnel files, and applicants can be asked to request them.

An appropriate question in an employment interview is to ask applicants what their supervisors would say if asked about them. If there is negative information, that question offers applicants an opportunity to tell their sides of the story. And the request for references may encourage applicants to convey all relevant information by forewarning them that they will be investigated.

Where to Check

For experienced applicants the most useful reference source is the previous employer, but recent lawsuits for defamation of character have made employers wary. Many companies require that all employment references come through the human resources department, which commonly limits responses to job title and dates of employment. But this information is useful. Getting dates from a series of employers may reveal gaps that the applicant has not reported.

Supervisors and associates have the most information about the applicant's skills and work habits. Some of them are more willing to share information than human resources professionals. Even if they have left the company, subordinates can be useful sources of information for the applicants with supervisory experience.

94

HOW TO AVOID NEGLIGENT HIRING

Mature adults often have connections in organizations where fellow members have useful information. Such organizations include professional and civic organizations and churches. These are often listed on résumés, and officers can be found even if the applicant has not named individuals in these groups.

Competitors, clients, customers, and vendors are in a position to give useful information for some applicants. Public records of conviction, judgments, mortgages, liens, and garnishees are appropriate to check where there are potential problems of security or financial responsibility.

Teachers, coaches, and guidance counselors of some high school graduates often have information relevant to employment, although extended checking may not be economical in the case of recent graduates applying for entry-level jobs. If intelligence and scholastic achievement are important for a particular job, the applicant can ask to have a transcript sent.

Colleges may be more important to check because of the level of the jobs involved. The importance of obtaining a transcript has been noted above. Professors may be able to provide useful information, especially if the student has been a laboratory assistant or teaching assistant. Information sources related to extracurricular activities include coaches, leaders of musical and drama groups, and staff members involved with student government.

Applicants often list pastors, neighbors, and friends as references. Usually these sources provide only a whitewash, and they are not worth contacting if adequate information is available from more objective sources. However, in the absence of a comprehensive picture from more appropriate sources, it may be worthwhile to try the personal references. Questions about where the applicant has worked or attended school may verify or complement other information. A useful question to a personal reference is "Who else knows this person?" That may lead to a whole new chain of inquiry.

How to Check

Most employment investigations are conducted by telephone. A telephone check is like an employment interview. The same subjects and techniques of questioning apply. *Government regulations also apply*. If the answers come at all, they come quickly. A

95

HOW TO HIRE WINNERS — LEGALLY

telephone conversation provides flexibility to ask for amplification or to follow up leads.

In the case of respondents who want to be sure of the identity of the caller, they can be invited to call back. If they require a release from the applicant, that can be mailed and the telephone call made after the release is received.

A generic telephone interview guide is given below.

TELEPHONE REFERENCE GUIDE

1. This is _____ of _____ Company. (Name of applicant) has applied to us for the position of _____, and I am calling to verify some information he/she had given us. What were the approximate dates of employment with your company?
_____

2. In what job did he/she start? _____
3. What other jobs did he/she hold?
_____

4. Would you please describe the duties of the last job?
_____

5. How well did he/she perform the job duties? If there was a formal performance appraisal, what was the rating?
_____

6. How was his/her attendance? _____
7. What were his/her earnings? _____
8. Why did he/she leave your company?
_____

9. What other reasons were there?
_____

10. What were his/her greatest strengths as an employee?
_____

11. What were the most significant weaknesses? _____

12. Do you know of any activities or circumstances outside of his/her employment that would have either a favorable or unfavorable effect on employment?
_____

13. Is there anything else you can tell me about this person's suitability for the position of _____
14. Would you rehire ? _____ If not, why not? _____
_____

The foregoing guide for reference checking is intended to suggest the points to cover rather than to be followed rigidly. Interviewers will be most effective if they use their own words and add clarifying or amplifying questions as necessary.

It is appropriate to add questions that are relevant for particular occupations. For example, inquiries about sales candidates could ask about total volume, new accounts, rank among other

HOW TO AVOID NEGLIGENT HIRING

salespersons, retention of old customers, and method of payment. Inquiries about managers could touch on number and type of people supervised, management style, budget responsibility, initiative, organizing ability, discipline, and relations with peers and higher management. For engineering and science applicants, questions might deal with problem solving, inventions, patents, ability to work independently, team work, and work habits.

Written inquiries take more time and yield less information, but some respondents will not provide information by telephone. Using the mail also offers an opportunity to send a release form. To make it easier for the respondent, written inquiries commonly include more checklists than open-ended questions. An example of a mailed reference form is given below.

APPLICANT REFERENCE CHECK

(name of applicant) has applied for the position of _____ with our company. Enclosed is a form signed by the applicant authorizing us to contact you for information about employment with your company. Your candid response will be greatly appreciated. If you would prefer to respond by telephone, we shall welcome your call to _____, 716-285-9671, ext. 375. All of the information will be treated as confidential.

Dates of employment : From _____ To _____

Job title and duties: _____

_____

Reason for leaving : _____

PLEASE CHECK THE APPROPRIATE BOX BELOW

	Below Average	Satisfactory	Above Average
Quality of Work			
Quantity of Work			
Teamwork			
Attendance			

Would you rehire? _____ If no, explain _____

Please add any other comments that will contribute to our employment decision.

97

HOW TO HIRE WINNERS — LEGALLY

A field investigation is best, but it is costly for most jobs. To an even greater extent than a telephone inquiry, a face-to-face interview permits flexibility and encourages frankness. When circumstances justify the cost, an employment specialist can make appointments with former employers or other informants and interview them in person. Another approach is to conduct the investigative interview over lunch.

In one field investigation the author spent a Saturday investigating a professional applicant living in a city 80 miles distant. Appointments were made to interview three of the applicant's graduate school professors at the conclusion of their Saturday faculty meeting. On the same trip interviews were scheduled at the homes of two people who had supervised the applicant in his most recent jobs, which he held while completing his graduate studies. In view of the generally favorable responses the applicant was visited in his home the same day, and a firm offer of employment was made, completing the whole transaction without loss of office time and with the promptness desirable in a competitive labor market.

An illustration of the way a field investigation can bring out information that is unavailable from other sources involves a management applicant whose resume described him as president of a company at a high salary. On paper his qualifications seemed excellent. Investigation disclosed that he had, indeed, been president of the corporation at the high salary he claimed. The corporation, however, was formed by an out-of-town syndicate for the sole purpose of stock trading, and the applicant was nothing more than a customer's man. He supervised only one secretary and had no experience with production, marketing, personnel work, or other management functions.

Who Should Investigate?

There is some advantage in having the investigation done by the same person who has conducted at least one of the employment interviews. It is easier to coordinate the information when it is all in one head. Detailed notes from an investigation may be more important than notes from an employment interview, even when the whole transaction is completed by the same person, but they are especially important if more then one person is involved.

People involved in the hiring process have an advantage if they participate in professional organizations and community

HOW TO AVOID NEGLIGENT HIRING

activities. Members of the Society for Human Resource Management, for example, may get acquainted in periodic meetings to an extent that makes them more candid in giving references. A first-name conversation on the telephone is likely to yield much more than a conversation between strangers.

Personnel investigations need not be limited to employment specialists. Heads of functional departments often establish personal relationships with their peers in professional societies for accountants, engineers, quality specialists, purchasing agents, technical writers, etc. Through their professional acquaintances, people in functional departments can sometimes contribute more to an investigation than the employment specialists.

Obtaining a credit report on an employment applicant has been a common practice, but that is now subject to several restrictions under the Fair Credit Reporting Act. In the first place, employers must tell the reporting agency why the report is requested and certify that the information will not be used for any other purpose. There are criminal penalties for violating this requirement. Names of credit reporting firms can be found in the yellow pages in any metropolitan phone book.

In addition to reporting credit history, some firms also provide "investigative consumer reports," based on information from neighbors and acquaintances. These longer reports include impressions of character, personal characteristics, and mode of living. Within three days of a request of this type of report the employer is required to inform the applicant that the report has been requested, regardless of whether the information is actually used. The applicant has a right to request a description of the nature and scope of the investigation.

The Fair Credit Reporting Act requires that if employment is denied in whole or in part on the basis of consumer report information, the employer must inform the applicant and give the name of the consumer reporting agency. This provision makes it possible for an applicant to correct any negative credit information, but it creates a new problem for the employer. If inaccurate information is corrected, the applicant can reapply for this job, but there are likely to be reasons for rejection in addition to the credit report. Employers can give themselves some protection by making it clear in their disclosure statements than the credit history was only one of several factors in the employment decision.

99

HOW TO HIRE WINNERS — LEGALLY

A few firms specialize in personnel investigations, which are not subject to the provisions of the Fair Credit Reporting Act if they do not include credit information. The applicant can be regarded as sufficiently informed by the common statement in application blanks that information provided by the applicant is subject to verification. Several firms have national coverage, which enables them to conduct in-person interviews and record checks anywhere in the country.

There are two advantages in using these services instead of having investigations done by employees of the recruiting company. One advantage is confidentiality. The company name is not revealed. A second advantage is that investigation is the main job of the investigators, and they can be expected to ask and record appropriate questions.

A disadvantage, however, is the cost, although it may not be more than the value of an employment specialist's time in a local investigation. A second disadvantage is that the field investigators work without supervision, and the quality control may be imperfect. With any investigation, no matter who conducts it, there is no guarantee of getting all relevant information.

Important negative information can be missed even by conscientious investigators. Selective personnel investigating firms are listed below:

Corporate Investigations, Inc. 1700 N. Highland Rd., Pittsburgh, PA 15241 (412) 831-2600.

Edge Information Management, Inc. 1901 S. Harbor City Blvd., Suite 401, Melbourne, FL 32901.

Equifax Security and Resource Management. 1600 Peachtree St., NW, Atlanta, GA 30309.

Employment Research Services (ERS). 800 827-2479.

Fidelifacts. 50 Broadway, New York, NY 10004 (212) 425-1520.

Gall & Gall. 4977 Northcutt Pl., Dayton, OH 45414 (513) 278-1645.

Investigations Corp. of America. 2964 Peachtree St., Atlanta, GA 30305.

National Employment Screening Service. 8801 S. Yale, Tulsa, OK 74137.

Pinkerton Investigation Services. 1-800-232-PINK (7465).

RefCheck Information Services. (614) 459-1442.

Information Resources. (310) 376-1399.

Records Search. 6191 Orange Dr., #6165H, Davie, FL 33314.

100

HOW TO AVOID NEGLIGENT HIRING

When any outside investigators are employed it is important that they comply with government regulations on discrimination. Violations could conceivable be charged to the recruiting company. The person authorizing the investigation is responsible for ascertaining that investigators are familiar with the regulations.

Interviewing Individual Informants

Investigative contacts with previous employers can focus directly on the applicant's work, but this is less suitable in interviewing other informants. Competitors, clients, and vendors can be asked about business or professional success and reputation, business ethics, and any employment history that is know. Set forth below are some questions that can be asked of informants not connected with the applicant's employment, such as acquaintances in community organizations, churches, and neighborhoods.

• How long have you known him/her? In what connection?

• How do you know about his/her work? Employer, job, length of time employed, job success and reputation.

• Where else has he/she worked? Employers, jobs, length of time employed, job success, reasons for changing jobs.

• What do you know about his/her work habits?

If responses include any hints of legal difficulties, or strengths and weaknesses related to employment, it may be possible to follow up with clarifying questions. However, direct questions about convictions, drinking, morals, or character could cause problems with EEO regulators.

In any interviewing related to hiring it is important to avoid leading questions. They can put words in an informant's mouth, leading to misinterpretation. It is also important to avoid *giving* information while *getting* information. A statement like "Are you familiar with his/her work at the Jones Company?" may be telling the informant something that the applicant does not want known.

101

HOW TO HIRE WINNERS — LEGALLY

Special Problems in Investigating

A few employers refuse to give out any reference information. One way of trying harder is to state that the applicant can't be hired unless the employment can be verified. That may break down some resistance. If a personnel clerk remains adamant, the chief executive officer may be more willing to violate policy.

Getting reference information from a current employer presents a sticky problem. One strategy is to ask the applicant for names of people who can verify information without jeopardizing the applicant's job security. This might be a coworker, but such a source cannot be expected to give any negative information. Another strategy is to make an offer of employment that is firm but subject to verification with the current employer. Applicants who expect a satisfactory reference can then resign and eliminate the problem. Those who are unwilling to do so may not be good risks.

Issues in Giving Information

Giving out certain information about present and former employees can leave an employer open to charges of defamation or libel. Both involve injuring a person by false statements. Defamation is oral; libel refers to something written. The truth of a statement represents a satisfactory defense in most instances, but there may be exceptions. Terms like "lazy . . . hostile . . . bad attitude . . . and stupid" are difficult to support with facts. Courts have awarded millions of dollars for defamation and libel.

Set forth below are guidelines for protecting a company from these kinds of lawsuits.

1. Centralize all reference giving. Communicate this firm policy to all employees, not only supervisors.
2. Stick to observable facts, like number of days absent.
3. Limit information to work-related items.
4. Obtain a written release from any employee leaving the company. Inform the employee what this release means.
5. Provide information only on a need-to-know basis. Casual inquiries are not answered, but a prospective employer has a legitimate need to know about job duties, skills, attendance, and dates of employment.

102

HOW TO AVOID NEGLIGENT HIRING

These guidelines for *giving* information contrast with the suggestions for seeking every source to *get* information. Which side of the fence you are on determines what is in your best interest.

chapter 8

HOW TO MINIMIZE LEGAL RISKS IN HIRING

SUMMARY OF LEGAL APPLICATIONS, RECRUITING, AND INTERVIEWING

Application Forms

Chapter 2 discusses legal issues in regard to questions asked on application forms. A brief review is set forth below.

Age: Most application forms do not call for age or date of birth. It is legal to ask if the applicant needs a work permit (if under 18).

Name: General questions about name change are illegal, but an applicant may be asked if any other names would be needed to check the work record.

Address: Birthplace and birthplace of parents may not be asked.

Citizenship: It is legal to ask only if the person has legal right to work in the United States; questions about naturalization are illegal.

Language: Questions about native language are illegal, but it is legal to ask about language proficiency.

Relatives: Questions about relatives are not illegal; it is legal to ask if any relatives are employed by this company, but it is illegal to use that information as a basis for rejection.

Arrests: Questions about arrests are illegal. For applicants for banking and retailing it is legal to ask about convictions for theft or embezzlement; general questions about convictions are questionable.

HOW TO HIRE WINNERS — LEGALLY

Military: The only legal question about military service is to ask if there is any military training or experience that would be useful on the job.

Hobbies and Organizations: General questions are illegal. It is legal to ask only if hobbies or organizational activities have contributed to job qualifications.

Education: Questions about schools attended are legal, but dates of attendance are not, because they usually reveal age.

Physical: It is only legal to ask if there are any physical limitations that would interfere with performing and identified job. General questions about physique and health are illegal.

Sex: The familiar "M" or "F" is illegal.

Race/Color: Such questions are clearly illegal.

Religion: Questions about religion are illegal. If weekend work is required of *all* employees, it may be legal to ask if applicants are available. However, employers are expected to make accommodations wherever possible for employees whose religion limits their availability for work Saturday and Sunday.

The foregoing restrictions derive primarily from the Civil Rights Act of 1964, which prohibits discrimination on the basis of sex, race, color, religion, and national origin.

Recruiting

On the basis of Executive Order 11246, enacted in 1965 and amended in 1968, firms with government contracts are required to take **affirmative action** to go out and seek members of the protected groups who are underrepresented in their work force. Reports to the government list the numbers of protected groups in the several job categories. If, for example, the number of minorities in skilled jobs is not up to expectation for the local population, an **affirmative action plan** must include steps to recruit more of the groups that are insufficiently represented. Failure to comply can result in loss of government contracts. Inspectors from the Office of Federal Contracts Compliance Programs make periodic visits to review status reports and affirmative action plans. OFCCP regulations apply to companies with government contracts or subcontracts of $10,000 or more.

106

HOW TO MINIMIZE LEGAL RISKS IN HIRING

The Viet Nam Era Veterans Readjustment Act of 1974 extended affirmative action requirements to veterans who served between 1964 and 1975 and to veterans with compensable disabilities of 30 per cent or more. Government contractors are required to take the following steps.

1. Recruit through the public employment service, Veterans Administration, and all veterans' counselors in agencies, service centers, and colleges.
2. Obtain advice and technical assistance from veterans' organizations.
3. Notify subcontractors and vendors of the company's affirmative action policy.
4. Train managers to fulfill their affirmative action obligations.
5. Consider all qualified veterans for promotion from within the company.

Interviewing

The restrictions that apply to application forms also apply to employment interviews, as discussed at the beginning of this chapter. It is illegal to initiate general inquiries about age, birthplace, citizenship, native language, relatives, arrests, leisure activities, marital status, and health.

The interview is more flexible than an application form, however. If an interviewee brings up a point of information about any of the prohibited subjects, there is no legal restriction on asking clarifying questions. On the other hand, there is a basis for a charge of discrimination if applicants have reason to think that they have been rejected because of age, marital status, arrests, or birthplace.

Detroit Edison lost a discrimination case partly because interview judgments by untrained white interviewers resulted in adverse impact that could not be justified on any objective grounds. It was shown that interviewers made subjective judgments about appearance, dress, speech, and personality, with no guidelines on questioning or interpreting information.

Guidelines for interviewing disabled applicants can be obtained from Mainstream, 3 Bethesda Metro Center, Suite 830, Bethesda, MD 20814 (301) 654-2400.

107

HOW TO HIRE WINNERS — LEGALLY

The Americans with Disabilities Act of 1990

Health and Physical Condition

General questions about height, weight, and disabilities have been illegal on the basis of previous laws. The Americans with Disabilities Act of 1990 *prohibits* additional questions, including the following:

- Have you ever had or been treated for any of the following conditions? (followed by checklist)
- Please list any condition or diseases for which you have been treated in the past _____ years.
- Have you ever been hospitalized? If so, explain.
- Have you even been treated by a psychiatrist or psychologist? If so, for what condition?
- Have you ever been treated for any mental condition?
- Is there any health-related reason you may not be able to perform the job for which you are applying? (A legal approach is to provide a job description and ask if the applicant can perform the essential functions without accommodation.)
- Have you had a major illness in the last five years?
- How many days have you been absent from work in the last five years? (However, an employer may provide information about attendance requirements and ask if an applicant is able to meet them.)
- Are you taking prescribed drugs? (This question may be asked, however, prior to a physical examination after a job offer is made.)
- Have you ever been treated for drug addiction or alcoholism?
- Have you ever filed for workers' compensation?

Physical Examinations

Physical examinations may be required *after* an employment offer is made but only if it is required of *all* applicants for similar positions. If all job offers are in writing there is little basis for dispute about the firmness of a job offer.

Physical examinations under ADA are more demanding than before. The examining physician must be provided with detailed physical demands for all essential functions, such as:

108

HOW TO MINIMIZE LEGAL RISKS IN HIRING

Number of pounds lifted; how often

Vision

Hearing

Dexterity

Coordination

Bending

Walking

Temperature at work site

Toxic substances

Noise

For jobs with physical demands it is prudent to have a formal job analysis. At this writing there are at least two software programs that can help firms produce ADA-complaint job descriptions. They are:

CrossWalk, from VocData Services, Inc. P.O. Box 2099, Vancouver, WA 98668

Descriptions Write Now, Knowledge Point, 1311 Clegg Street, Petaluma, CA 94954.

A *Technical Assistance Manual* is available from EEOC.

Among books on the ADA are three published by the Society for Human Resource Management:

The Americans With Disabilities Act, by Michael J. Lotito, Michael J. Soltis, and Richard Pimentel.

The Americans With Disabilities Act: Making the ADA Work For You, by Richard Pimentel, Michael J. Lotito, and Francis P. Alvares.

What Managers and Supervisors Need to Know About The ADA, by Michael J. Lotito, Richard Pimentel, and Denise Bissonnette.

Medical examinations can be unrestricted, but an applicant with a disability may not be rejected unless the reason for rejection is related to the "essential functions" of the job. However, employers are safer from unwarranted assumptions by regulators if they only possess information that is relevant to the "es-

HOW TO HIRE WINNERS — LEGALLY

sential functions," and the examining physician should be instructed appropriately, with a written statement of essential functions. The physician's report should instructed appropriately, with a written statement of essential functions. The entire medical record remains with the physician and not in the company personnel files. An independent physician has more credibility with regulators than a physician employed by the company.

All medical information, even when it is limited to essential functions, should be placed in a confidential medical file, accessible only to five sources:

1. Supervisors who need to know about work restrictions and accommodations.
2. First aid and safety personnel when emergency treatment might be required.
3. Compliance investigators.
4. Courts and compensation claim records.
5. Other sources with the written consent of the employee or applicant.

Increased liability and increased health insurance costs for a disabled applicant are not legal grounds for rejection, but any applicants, including disabled ones, can be rejected if they pose a threat to the health and safety of themselves and other workers. Such a threat must be capable of documentation. Severity and imminence of the threat are considerations.

Drug Testing

A test to determine illegal use of drugs is not considered a medical examination, and such a test is specifically permitted under the ADA. A current user of illegal drugs is not considered disabled under the law and is not protected by it. However, the law protects persons who have successfully completed drug rehabilitation programs and are no longer using. An employer may enforce a prohibition regarding use of alcohol and illegal drugs in the workplace.

To minimize legal challenges it is important for employers to have written policies regarding pre-employment drug testing and to treat all applicants consistently. Some state and local laws may differ from federal regulations, which are discussed here, and it is important to comply with any laws. The right to test applicants for jobs involving public safety, as in the case of bus

110

HOW TO MINIMIZE LEGAL RISKS IN HIRING

drivers, has generally been upheld. Claims of privacy invasion can be minimized if applicants are informed in advance of a drug testing requirement. Permitting rescheduling a test is undesirable, because a substance abuser could refrain from use for a time. In case of positive test results it is only fair to repeat the test using the same sample. Samples must be kept in the physician's office for 180 days in case of litigation. Maintaining confidentiality requires that results of positive tests be kept only in the physician's office. The applicant is the only one informed of the results, expect that a code can be used on a personnel record to indicate test failure.

Current employees may be tested after accidents and if there is other "possible cause." Random testing of employees has been upheld if it is related to public safety, but a computer programmer won an award of $485,000 after she was fired for refusing to take a random urinalysis[1]. Her case rested on the principle of right of privacy.

Persons covered by the ADA include those with a "physical" or mental impairment that substantially limits one or more of the major life activities . . . such as walking, seeing, hearing, learning, or speaking. Employers are not required to hire people just because they have disabilities. Better qualified nondisabled applicants may be given preference, but employers are required to make "reasonable accommodation" for qualified applicants who have disabilities. A general definition of reasonable accommodation is not possible, but it could include installing a wheelchair ramp, widening office aisles, or providing a stool to reduce standing. A list of possible accommodations may be obtained from the Equal Employment Opportunity Commission, 1801 L Street N.W., Washington, DC.

The ADA law took effect July 26, 1992 for employers of 25 persons or more. For employers of 15-24 persons the effective date is July 26, 1994. Employers of fewer than 15 employees are not subject to the law.

Several government programs are specially designed to promote the employment of individuals with disabilities or other special qualifications. These include disabled veterans, Viet Nam

---

[1] Hafner, Katie & Garland, Susan, "Testing for Drug Use: Handle with care, *Business Week,* March 28, 1988.

111

HOW TO HIRE WINNERS — LEGALLY

era veterans individuals, eligible for Targeted Job Tax Credits, and individuals eligible for Job Training Partnership Act assistance. For applicants in these categories it is legal and perhaps necessary to inquire about disabilities.

Resources for Employing People with Disabilities

A subscription to Managing Diversity can provide current information on hiring the disabled—P.O. Box 819, Jamestown, NY 14702.

The Job Accommodation Network is a free information service located at West Virginia University, P.O. Box 6122, Morgantown, WV 26506. It offers guidelines for accommodations.

The Foundation on Employment and Disability provides a hotline in at least seven languages at (301) 214-8861.

The National Institute on Disability and Rehabilitation Research offers information and technical assistance for employers. Part of the U.S. Department of Education, its number is (202) 205-8134.

IBM National Support Center for Persons With Disabilities offers advice on computer-assisted devices for disabled persons. Telephone (800) IBM - 2133, voice and TDD.

AT&T National Accessible Communication Products has a variety of communication devices for persons with disabilities. (800) 233 - 1222 or TDD.

The Assistive Technology Access Center of Digital Equipment Corporation in Norwood, MA can be reached at (503) 351-4570.

A computer program teaching ABC's of ADA is available from the Wonderlic testing organization at (800) 323-3742.

Psychological Tests

The government's 1978 **Uniform Guidelines On Employee Selection Procedures** apply to any selection procedures, and there are penalties and liabilities for adverse impact on any protected group.

In the first landmark case under Title VII of the Civil Rights Act of 1964 (*Griggs v. Duke Power*, 1971) an intelligence test and a

112

HOW TO MINIMIZE LEGAL RISKS IN HIRING

mechanical aptitude test screened out a disproportionate number of black applicants, and a class action suit was filed. The court found that the company had not provided any evidence that the tests were job related. Neither was the requirement of high school diploma demonstrated to be job related.

In two other lawsuits regarding discrimination on the basis of test scores, courts upheld the attempted validation study relating test scores to success in a police academic training program, even though a disproportionate number of black applicants was rejected.

The State of Connecticut thought that it avoided charges of discrimination when it made sure that, after a multi-step selection process, it promoted 23 percent of black and 14 percent of whites. However, in the case of *Connecticut v. Teal* (1992) the court found that a much lower percentage of blacks passed a preliminary written examination and were eliminated. The bottom line did not represent the entire process.

Possibilities for the validity of tests rest on their job relatedness. In the case of simulations or job samples the relatedness is demonstrated by job analysis, as in the case of a keyboard test to select word processors. When the relationship is less clear, as in the case of an intelligence test, the introduction of a testing program should be preceded by a decision about the measures of job success that the tests are designed to predict, and a validation study should be planned. That requires quantified ratings that clearly differentiate good performers from poor performers.

Testing has often been abandoned because companies selected to top scorers, in descending order, resulting in disparate impact. When a battery of tests is used, it is appropriate to consider all the scores, along with education, work experience, and references. Using one test or procedure for preliminary screening can result in adverse impact. That is why Connecticut lost its case. Possibilities for avoiding discrimination charges are reduced when all selection information, as well as goals of a diverse work force, is considered in making sound and defensible hiring decisions.

Educational Requirements

An earlier chapter noted that hardly any job requires a college degree, but in the case of *Sporlock v. United Airlines* (1972) a degree requirement was upheld. On the basis of evidence that

113

HOW TO HIRE WINNERS — LEGALLY

only 9 of 5,900 flight officers were black, Spurlock charged that the requirements of a degree and 500 hours of flight time were discriminatory. However, United won the case by showing that a degree indicated that the applicant had the ability to learn in a classroom, which was important because of the intensive refresher courses required every 6 months.

The Numbers Game

The OFCCP has been sympathetic to statistical evidence that fewer minorities are employed in the more desirable jobs. However, a discrimination suit based on disparate numbers was lost in the Ward's Cove case (1989). In an Alaska fishery it was shown that all white collar employees were Caucasian, while all the low-skill employees were Filipino or members of other minorities. The plaintiffs lost, however, because they failed to prove that the numbers resulted from any discriminatory practice. The Supreme Court ruled that it was sufficient for the company to show that its practices "served" its business goals.

Previous court decisions had ruled that "business necessity" had to be shown by a company using any procedures that resulted in disparate impact.

THE CIVIL RIGHTS ACT OF 1991

As a result of the Ward's Cove decision and other decisions by the conservative Reagan court, Congress passed the Civil Rights Act of 1990 to reduce the disadvantage to complainants and restore the rules applying before Ward's Cove. However, President Bush vetoed the Act, claiming that it would result in hiring quotas because employers would find it too difficult to defend their practices.

In 1991 Congress tried again, and finally a compromise with the President was reached, resulting in the new act becoming effective November 21, 1991. The employer again has the burden of proving that disparate impact on minorities in hiring is job related and is consistent with business necessity. One aspect of the compromise was to include a provision that the complaining party has the burden of demonstrating that a particular employment practice or combination of practices caused the disparate impact.

114

HOW TO MINIMIZE LEGAL RISKS IN HIRING

A new provision for jury trials remains in the act. Damages are limited to cases of *intentional* discrimination, excluding unintentional disparate impact. Compensatory and punitive damages are available, but they are capped at $50,000 per individual for employers with 15-100 employees, up to $300,000 per individual for employers with more than 500 employees.

Because of past discrimination, consent degrees or court orders require hiring preferences for minorities, as in the cases of firemen and policemen in certain cities. The 1991 act leaves these agreements in place.

Race norming on the General Aptitude Test Battery of the Department of Labor was started in an effort to make more minority referrals by comparing test scores only within groups of whites or blacks. That practice is now prohibited.

Title II of the 1991 act establishes a commission to crack the "glass ceiling" by focusing "greater attention on the limited importance of eliminating artificial barriers to the advancement of women and minorities to management and decision-making positions in business." The commission will make an annual award for excellence in promoting a more diverse skilled work force at the management and decision-making levels in business.

Overturning another Supreme Court decision, the 1991 act extends protection of U.S. anti-discrimination laws to U.S. citizens employed overseas by U.S. companies. However, the act does provide that an employer cannot be required to violate laws of the host country.

Experience Requirements

It is legal to *prefer* applicants with relevant work experience, but an arbitrary *requirement* to two years or 10 years of experience can create problems in two ways. It might discriminate against women who have been out of the work force for child rearing. It might also discriminate against minorities. People with more experience than the specified number might be over 40 and thus protected by age discrimination laws, which apply to applicants between the ages of 40 and 70. It is illegal to require that applicants for entry jobs meet the requirements for promotional jobs.

115

HOW TO HIRE WINNERS — LEGALLY

Legal Activities Laws

Several states have enacted legislation prohibiting employers from discriminating against employees or applicants because of legal off-the-job activities. In New York, for example, it is now illegal in hiring, promotion, or retention to discriminate against employees because of political activities, legal recreational activities, legal use of a consumable products (like tobacco), or exercise of rights under labor laws.

Job Analysis

Job descriptions and person specifications based on job analysis not only diminish the vulnerability to lawsuits, but they also represent sound professional practice. This has become even more important to comply with the Americans with Disabilities Act of 1990.

Interviewers

It is important to train interviewers not only in how to question for information but also in how to avoid questions that leave them open to charges of discrimination. They also need to avoid promises that can be interpreted as implied contracts.

Reference Checks

Questioning in reference checks is subject to the same legal restrictions as employment interviewing, and information from references is subject to privacy laws.

Records

Government regulations require companies to keep records of the EEO status of applicants and hires. For hiring, annual determination of adverse impact should be made for any groups that constitute more than two percent of the applicants. Comparisons of males versus females and blacks versus whites must be made, but the regulations do not require analysis of each subgroup, like black females.

Taking pity on smaller employers (less than 100 employees), the government does not require them to make adverse impact determinations.

116

HOW TO MINIMIZE LEGAL RISKS IN HIRING

Negligent Hiring

Appropriate questioning and checking are required for any applicant who has an opportunity or likelihood of actions like assault or theft that would affect other employees, customers, visitors, or clients.

Hiring Decisions

Hiring decisions need to be defensible. There is no legal problem when one white male engineering manager is hired instead of another while male, provided that there are defensible requirements for an engineering degree and some years of experience. Many hiring decisions are like that, and tests or other procedures may be used, because white males are not members of a protected class.

Similarly, there is no problem when a white female secretary is hired instead of another white female. There would be no grounds for discrimination on the basis of sex. However, if black females are in the applicant pool (and they should be in urban areas), a rejected black may have grounds for a discrimination charge unless she fails to meet qualifications in spelling, filing skills, or typing speed that have been firmly established instead. On the other hand, a rejected black applicant would have no grounds for a discrimination charge if a black applicant with higher qualifications is hired.

The basis for legal challenges is minimized when recruitment yields applicant pools that include qualified representatives of the protected groups.

Reverse Discrimination

Charges of reverse discrimination have been filed in some employment situations, particularly in cases of firefighters and law enforcement officers, where past discrimination has led to agreements to hire a higher percentage of minorities. At this writing in 1992 the legal status of such quotas has not been settled with certainty. However, in one case the Supreme Court clearly decided that race could be considered in selection if it were not the only criterion. That was in the case of a medical school applicant named Bakke, who was denied admission despite scoring higher on a test than some black applicants. Bakke won his case

HOW TO HIRE WINNERS — LEGALLY

and was admitted because the medical school had established a rigid quota, based only on race. However, the court ruled that race could have been considered legally along with other criteria, including test scores.

The Four-Fifths Rule.

The Uniform Selection Guidelines of the government offer a rule of thumb that organizations can use to determine adverse impact. The ratio of any protected group must be at least 80 percent of the ratio of the favored group. For example if 60 of 120 white applicants for a particular type of job are hired, and there are 100 black applicants for the same job, then hiring 40 of the black applicants would leave the firm in compliance.

A smaller hiring ratio for blacks gives an initial suspicion of discrimination, but that, in itself, does not constitute a violation. There is no illegal discrimination if not enough minority applicants meet well-defined selection criteria.

This raises a question about Who Is An Applicant? Applicants must be counted if they respond to advertising, but it may not be necessary to count people who make "shotgun" inquiries by telephone or by sending in unsolicited résumés when no suitable job is open. Employers who want to minimize their exposure to discrimination charges can refuse to accept walk-in applications when there is no job opening, and they can return applications that are mailed in.

STRATEGIES FOR COMPLIANCE

The foregoing sections of this chapter suggest ways to avoid adverse impact on protected groups in making hiring decisions. Validation of selection procedures is desirable for personnel management, but the government requires evidence of validity **ONLY WHEN THERE IS ADVERSE IMPACT** in hiring, promotion, retention, or transfer. Adverse impact is determined by bottom line numbers.

When the numbers of persons and differences in selection rates are small, it is reasonable to assume that some differences among groups could occur by chance, and the government will not necessarily require a validation study.

118

HOW TO MINIMIZE LEGAL RISKS IN HIRING

Bottom line evidence of selection ratios refers to the total selection process, including application forms, interviews, and reference checks. It is important, however, to make sure that there is no adverse impact at any stage that prevents applicants from proceeding through subsequent stages, as in the case of *Connecticut v. Teal*.

As the Supreme Court determined in the Bakke case, employers can consider race and gender to meet affirmative action goals, so long as a rigid quota is not established. Bakke won his reverse discrimination case because he was excluded by a quota. In the total selection process many employers will strive for diversity in their work forces. They can avoid discrimination charges if they hire enough of the protected groups. It behooves each employer to have a rationale for each hiring decision. That rationale can include experience, interview impressions, tests results, reference checks, and even affirmative action. Sound person specifications and broad recruiting help to provide an applicant pool from which effective and defensible hiring decisions can be made. There is no way to achieve complete protection from litigation, but risk is minimized if there is no adverse impact and there is sound rationale for each hiring decision.

When a charge of adverse impact is made it is important to obtain the services of someone who knows the regulations and is competent in validation strategies. A state-licensed industrial psychologist is likely to have appropriate qualifications, and others may have them. A human resources generalist can ask the following questions of an employee or prospective consultant.

1. How should we respond to the charge or inquiry?
2. What measures of job success (criteria) can we use or develop?
3. How can we show the relationship between each of our selection procedures and the measure(s) of job success?
4. What will such a study cost?
5. Is it worth it, or should we just drop the challenged procedure?
6. If you suggest a validation study, what strategy will you use, Content, Construct, or Criterion-Related? Why?

A competent specialist should be able and willing to explain any technical terms. Following are some explanations intended for an informed consumer of specialized services. They are not technical enough to provide full competency for a nonspecialist.

119

HOW TO HIRE WINNERS — LEGALLY

Content Validation

A job analysis for a word processing job will show that keyboard skills are required. A keyboard skills test derives from a job *content* and may be used for selection. Validation consists in demonstrating that the content of the test is representative of a specified percentage of the word processor's job. Suggestions for content-based tests were offered in Chapter 6.

Criterion-Related Validation

A job analysis for machinist apprentices is likely to show that success requires a certain level of general intelligence and mechanical aptitude. Continued legal use of such tests for selecting apprentices requires that they show positive correlation with an appropriate measure of job success. This relationship must be statistically significant to an extent that would occur by chance not more than five times in 100 ($p < .05$). The relevant measure of job sucess might be grades in training classes, number of weeks required to develop a specified skill, number of rejects on a specified production job, time to set up a machine for production, experts rating of quality of products, etc. The statistical procedures apply only when sufficient numbers of employees are involved. Thirty is bare minimum, and 100 is a more comfortable number. There is also the issue of correlating ratings of current employees with their test scores at the time of hiring (concurrent validation) or testing applicants for a period of time, and then correlating their scores with ratings after six months "criterion contamination," which means that supervisors making any subjective rating do not have access to the test scores of the employees. Criterion-related validation can be fairly expensive, which is the reason that firms have sometimes dropped pre-employment testing.

Synthetic Validity

In many companies only one or two people are hired in a year, not enough to meet the statistical requirements for a criterion-related validation study. In such cases "synthetic validity" can be investigated. For example, job analysis might reveal that a component of mechanical aptitude is required for machinists, tool makers, maintenance mechanics, and millwrights. If appropriate measures of job success can be identified, numbers of employees from the different jobs can be combined and correlated with the pre-employment test scores.

120

HOW TO MINIMIZE LEGAL RISKS IN HIRING

"Validity generalization" involves a similar procedure for using a validation study in one company to justify a program of testing for an almost identical job in another company. Validity generalization depends on the close correspondence between the job analyses in the different companies. The courts are likely to take an especially close look at any validation studies based on synthetic validity and validity generalization, which require sophisticated procedures.

Construct Validity

Sophisticated procedures are also required to establish "construct validity." "Construct" in this sense (accent on the first syllable) refers to an aspect of job performance that is found in more than one job, as determined by research studies. For example, a study of accidents might find that crane operators and drivers of automobiles who have accidents have a lower level of eye-hand coordination than the average person. If so, we could define a construct of "eye-hand coordination." Using a test of eye-hand coordination for selecting bus drivers would be defensible, but legal use of such a test would require convincing a court. Other constructs that could be considered include creativity, organizing ability, and persuasiveness. All are difficult to define and test, which is the reason that the construct validity approach is more often used in psychological research than in responding to a charge of discrimination.

Legal Counsel

For any company it is prudent to have a qualified lawyer review all components of a personnel selection program and to advise when any changes are considered. Of course a lawyer as well as an industrial psychologist is required if a charge of discrimination is filed.

However, not many lawyers are familiar with laws and regulations relating to hiring and discrimination. A human resources consultant may be more familiar. In seeking legal counsel it is appropriate to ask prospective counsel if he/she is familiar with the statute or regulation under which a charge is brought and to ask about the prospective lawyer's experience with similar cases. If the lawyer is not familiar with the issues, it is appropriate to ask for referral to a lawyer more experienced in the issues at hand. In urban areas a lawyer reference service can be useful.

121

HOW TO HIRE WINNERS — LEGALLY

Keep Current

Employment laws are subject to change, particularly in state legislatures. Employers can protect themselves by subscribing to a service that publishes continual updates. They can also benefit from subscribing to appropriate professional journals and participating in professional organizations.

One useful source is Part 1607 - Uniform Guidelines on Employee Selection Procedures, printed in the *Federal Register,* Friday, August 25, 1978.

A second source is Chapter XIV - Equal Employment Opportunity Commission - Adoption of Questions and Answers designed to clarify and provide a common interpretation of the Uniform Guidelines printed in the *Federal Register,* Friday, March 2, 1979.

Both these publications are free. I obtained my copies from my Congressional representative.

REFERENCES

Hafner, Katie, and Garland, Susan, "Testing for Drug Use: Handle with Care." *Business Week*, March 28, 1988

chapter 9

HOW TO MAKE SURE YOU HIRE WINNERS

WHAT CAN GO WRONG

1. The most basic element in recruiting and selecting employees comes at the beginning. That is the person specifications derived from a job analysis and job description. They can be informal, but hiring the most appropriate employee depends on clearly defining what kind of person is needed. Too often the job description is not updated or it was never very clear in the first place.

2. Recruiting is not always done in the best places. It is too easy for some employers to depend on walk-ins or to limit advertising to the local newspaper. Unskilled laborers, managers, nurses, and chemists are not necessarily found through the same sources. It is important to determine what prospective recruiters read or listen to or where they have contacts.

3. Application blanks provide all the information necessary for employment decisions only if they are thoughtfully designed. More than one type of application blank may be required to elicit skills in the skilled trades, patents and publications of researchers, and accomplishments of sales workers.

4. Employment interviews contribute usefully to employment decisions only if they get applicants to talk enough and reveal their motivation, intellectual ability, and interpersonal skills while explaining their accomplishments, difficulties, and career development. Usually training is required for effective interviewing.

HOW TO HIRE WINNERS — LEGALLY

5. Reference checking, or more accurately, "personnel investigating," may not be done at all, or it may be limited to verification of the last employment. Avoiding a hiring mistake or "negligent hiring" depends on making sure that all time periods are covered and that any questions about abilities and relationships are resolved.

6. Poor coordination of the hiring process can result in hiring mistakes. Avoiding such mistakes requires clarification of selection criteria and agreement on criteria by all the people involved in the hiring decision.

7. Trying to match a present or previous employee, or "cloning," can result in a hiring mistake. A machinist can be effective without matching the education, experience, or physical characteristics of a predecessor. Short salesmen can be as effective as tall ones, and women can be as effective as men in most jobs.

8. It is difficult for managers to hire people stronger than they are. But an organization may not be able to grow unless that is done. In the best organizations some employees advance beyond the managers who hired them.

9. The "halo effect" of attractive appearance, extensive vocabulary, several inventions, or opening new markets may cause a hiring manager to overlook questionable motivation, interpersonal conflicts, or an excessive amount of customer complaints.

10. The impact of previous applicants often has an inappropriate effect on hiring decisions. A common error is to hire an applicant who is slightly better than several predecessors even though that applicant is not fully qualified. Employers who give up on finding a fully qualified person usually make a mistake, provided that their person specifications are sound. Pressure to fill the job may result in a hiring decision based on hope rather than objective judgment.

HOW TO MAKE SURE YOU HIRE WINNERS

11. Biases and stereotypes often lead to inappropriate hiring decisions. Some managers are biased for or against graduates of certain colleges, fat people, short people, women, African-Americans, or people from the Middle West. Sound hiring requires looking at the individual, without undue influence from the individual's race, religion, sex, physical characteristics, or institutional affiliations.

12. The fit between the individual and the organizational culture is important to consider, independent of the job description. People who fit comfortably into a bureaucratic organization are misfits in a fastgrowing, participatory organization. The applicant's fit with the boss may also be more important than the skills involved. The differences of opinion encouraged by some bosses can't be tolerated by others.

Organizing for Hiring Decisions

1. Understanding person specifications, hiring criteria, and agreement on them are important for everyone participating in the hiring process.

2. Effective management of the hiring process requires:

   a. Agreement on who has responsibility for each element.

   b. Screening out applicants who are clearly unqualified.

   c. Designating a host for applicants.

   d. Scheduling interviews realistically and appropriately.

   e. Sharing information and impressions systematically, perhaps with the use of an evaluation form.

   f. Clarifying who makes final decisions, the department manager, a group that strives for consensus, a majority of some group, or a top manager.

HOW TO HIRE WINNERS — LEGALLY

What Contributes to Hiring Decisions

A *résumé* is an applicant's advertising piece. It tells what the applicant wants employers to know and omits unfavorable information, but it commonly includes interpretable elements nevertheless.

Job skills and accomplishments are shown in a résumé. They may be distorted or exaggerated, but they are usually based on some facts. Education, unless it is falsified, can be interpreted. The applicant's presentation of sequence of jobs may reflect stability, career planning, and the types of work settings preferred by the applicant.

Appropriately designed *application blanks* can show more than resumes. They can include reasons for taking jobs, reasons for leaving, income, persons to contact for references, major accomplishments, and difficulties or weaknesses.

An *employment interview* can clarify and amplify information in application blanks and résumés. It also yields impressions of appearance, poise, language skills, and interpersonal skills. It may also produce more information on motivation and career development. There may be clues about the applicant's fit with the boss and the culture of the organization.

A *personnel investigation* can yield information about honesty, attendance, skills, accomplishments, weaknesses, concealed elements in the applicant's background, and interpersonal skills and conflicts. It also verifies the applicant's claims of dates and types of employment.

Psychological tests can provide more accurate measures of intelligence than other sources. They may also provide information about special skills and abilities, such as mechanical aptitude, clerical aptitude, and aptitude for computer programming or word processing. Clues about accuracy of résumé information may also emerge. For example, one applicant claimed a BSME from Massachusetts Institute of Technology, which implied a high level of intelligence. However, he ranked in the lowest tenth of engineering graduates on each of two mechanical reasoning tests and in the lowest tenth of management applicants on an intelligence test. Personality tests showed strong status needs, which might explain falsifying his application. His education could have

HOW TO MAKE SURE YOU HIRE WINNERS

been checked, but the unfavorable test results were sufficient reason for rejecting him without bothering to investigate further. In the case of a female or minority applicant, however, verification of the background would be more important to avoid legal difficulties.

Developing Selection Criteria

Prior to a recruiting campaign, a pharmaceutical company asked managers to write descriptions of their best sales reps. One of these descriptions follows:

> One of the most important things he does when he begins a program of promotion of a new item is to become thoroughly convinced with all aspects of therapeutics surrounding this item.

> His *product knowledge* is such that there are very few questions asked of him in a doctor's office that he cannot answer, and, in so doing, he conveys confidence to the physician—a very important attribute.

> This man represents no problem as to *motivation* since he is able, because of his own *enthusiasm*, to keep himself highly motivated at all times. He follows the prescribed methods, as to proper sequence of pertinent facts in his sales presentations, and intermingles with these facts an *originality* which lends itself to his being able to present a *highly interesting* presentation. This work is very closely akin to *showmanship*, which he is able to interject into his work in such a way that he, at no time, appears to be of the "showoff" type.

Descriptions of other successful sales reps include *personal appearance, eager to learn, alert, good speaking voice,* and *prepared*, in addition to repeating characteristics mentioned in the preceding paragraph.

Mobil Chemical hired a consulting firm to conduct a more elaborate survey of their exemplary employees, focusing on "competencies" shared by the most successful persons. They looked at skills, knowledge, social role, self-image, traits, and motives. Valid predictors of success throughout the organization included Concern for Effectiveness, Enthusiasm for Work, Self-Confidence,

127

HOW TO HIRE WINNERS — LEGALLY

Initiative, Communication Skills, Thinking Ability, Flexibility, and Interpersonal Relations.

University of Michigan professor David Ulrich, in a journal article, described one company that invites customers to suggest criteria for selecting sales representatives. Then those customers review the résumés of applicants and have input into hiring decisions. That process gives the customer a stake in the sales rep's success, and the subsequent relationship is predisposed to be profitable.

What To Look For In Applicants

Throughout résumés, application blanks, interviews, and reference information there are bits of information relating to selection criteria. Set forth below are examples of information that can be interpreted favorably or unfavorably.

CRITERIA FOR ALL APPLICANTS

Intelligence: Education completed. Oral and written English. Organization of ideas. Educational and cultural references.

Reliability: Length of time of jobs. Failure of any school subjects. Level of responsibility. Report of completing assignments.

Interpersonal Relations: Mention of relationships in jobs and school, fraternal organizations. Comments about supervisors and associates. Jobs that involve interaction.

CRITERIA FOR MANAGERS

Leadership: Captain or president in school, college, and community organizations. Selected for managing or coordinating responsibility at work. Mention of associates coming for advice.

Organizing Ability: Mention of organizing projects and activities to successful completion in work, school, and community. Balance between focusing on overall picture or details. Interview answers too sketchy or too detailed.

HOW TO MAKE SURE YOU HIRE WINNERS

Achievement Drive: Statement of goals. Believable or verified accomplishments. Advancement at work.

Decisiveness: Career decisions. Reports of decision making at work. Prompt and targeted answers in the interview.

Initiative: Mention of taking charge of activities. Championing new products. Starting a business. Volunteering information.

CRITERIA FOR SALES

Motivation: Goals include money and improved status. Preference of being rewarded in proportion to efforts.

Energy: Participation in sports. Regular work-outs. Working long hours. Moonlighting.

Confidence: Makes own decisions. Tries new things. Doesn't need advice. Expects to succeed in tasks attempted.

Competitiveness: Winning is important. Keeps track of success in relation to peers.

Relationships: Likes to meet people but can do without their affection.

Listening skills: Quick response and rapport. Smoothly initiates conversation.

Risk-Taking: Takes risks for rewards in business and sports. May gamble.

Optimism: Sees the doughnut instead of the hole. Expects to close the next sale. Expects tomorrow to be better. Not fazed by moderate loss or failure.

INDEPENDENT PROFESSIONALS

Independence: Solves own problems. Made career plans independently. Studied alone. Worked on independent projects. Accepts responsibility.

Creativity: Invented or developed something independently.

Results Oriented: Completes tasks. Clearly defines goal and persists until it is reached. Patient in working through difficult problems.

A Case Study

A unique and comprehensive selection system at the Toyota plant in Georgetown, Kentucky was described in an article in *HR Magazine* for March 1990 by Chuck Cosentino, John Allen, and Richard Williams. Toyota's emphasis on teamwork required hiring people who could fit comfortable into that non traditional organization.

Through initial discussions with managers Toyota identified selection criteria, including acceptance of responsibility, ability to work with others, and leadership competencies usually associated with supervisors. Job analyses also identified need for problem solving, initiative, and oral communication skills.

Jobs were listed in all of Kentucky's public employment offices, and applicants completing Toyota's application forms were given a fact sheet explaining Toyota's values and expectations. They also saw an orientation video. No candidates were eliminated on the basis of application forms.

Skills assessment was accomplished with the Job Service's General Aptitude Test Battery (GATB). A specially designed inventory was used to assess motivation to work in a participative environment. Maintenance skills were also tested. Participation in an Interpersonal Assessment Center required eight hours to complete. This included a group discussion exercise, a problem-solving exercise, and a simulation of assembly work involving output, speed, and ideas for improvement. Survivors of the preceding selection steps completed a Leadership Assessment Center, including an in-basket and assessment of counseling and scheduling abilities. Hands-on tests were administered to maintenance applicants; trained line managers conducted interviews. Applicants completing all these steps were given drug and alcohol tests as well as physical examinations.

Toyota reports a low five percent turnover rate and two percent absenteeism, with productivity ahead of schedule. Toyota is

HOW TO MAKE SURE YOU HIRE WINNERS

not the only organization using a comprehensive selection system with several kinds of assessment, but Toyota's may be the most extensive, with the greatest number of applicants.

Comment: Toyota's approach may have been influenced not only by its need to select team members but also by its need for public relations. They did not eliminate applicants at early stages, and their simulations probably had face validity.

Their efforts to establish criteria in advance represent sound professional practice. The same comment can be made for having line managers conduct interviews after training.

In the Kentucky labor market it may have been sufficient to recruit only through the public employment service, but many companies would need to recruit skilled workers and managers through other sources. The orientation video and fact sheet probably were important as introductions to this nontraditional corporate culture, but they would be less necessary in traditional business.

In most circumstances many applicants could be eliminated on the basis of well-designed application forms. Likewise, interpersonal assessments and leadership assessments would be less necessary in recruitment for traditional companies. The hands-on tests for maintenance applicants have more potential value and less risk of discrimination charges than other means of testing, but they are expensive.

In other circumstances screening interviews could be used, and personality testing could be substituted for some of the assessment center procedures.

In a selection system of this complexity it is highly probable that some of the elements do not contribute significantly to prediction of job success. A study relating each selection element with measure of success and adjustment of the job would be likely to permit elimination of some of the selection steps.

Review of Steps in Recruiting and Selecting

1. Job analysis, job description, person specifications.

2. Analysis of possible recruitment sources.

HOW TO HIRE WINNERS — LEGALLY

3. Placing advertising.

4. Informal recruitment steps, such as networking.

5. Reviewing résumés and/or application forms.

6. Training interviewers.

7. Scheduling interviews.

8. Testing when appropriate.

9. Reference checking.

10. Bringing all information together for hiring decisions.

11. Making offers, subject to physical exams when necessary.

12. Informing candidates who are not selected.

POSTSCRIPT

The employees of an organization determine its effectiveness, its culture, and its attractiveness. This book presents state-of-the-art information and techniques needed to hire the best people available. It shows how to do that within the constraints of laws and regulations.

Sound hiring is a necessary but insufficient condition for the prosperity of an organization. Appropriate orientation of new employees is needed to adapt them into an organization's culture. That does not happen automatically. New employees also need training, even when they have sound basic qualifications. After initial training they need regular coaching to meet the expectations of supervisors. They need retraining when conditions change, and they need cross training to increase their value for themselves and for the employer.

Employees seldom function well unless they have supportive supervision. Supervisors may have more effect on performance that the aptitudes of individual employees. Supervision is the most critical element in morale. Compensation plans can motivate or demotivate. Competitive benefits are needed not only for humanitarian reasons but also to retain employees. Career opportunities are needed to motivate the best employees.

Change is constant in labor market conditions, in laws affecting employment, in record-keeping technology, in testing technology, and in the education of new employees. People responsible for hiring decisions need to keep abreast of all conditions that affect their work.

Total Quality Management is a current system for making optimum use of a work force. Other approaches may emerge in the future, while TQM goes the way of quality circles, Theory y, and time-and-motion study. Effective managers will continually update their knowledge. They can start with hiring quality people, using the knowledge and techniques described in this book.

INDEX

A

Advertising 9–12
Affirmative action 18–19
Americans with Disabilities Act (ADA) 6, 108–112
Application forms 24, 28–33, 45–46, 105–106
Aptitudes 80–81
Assessment Centers 85–87

C

Civil Rights Act 114–115
Compliance 34, 118–119

D

Disabilities 108–112
Dictionary of Occupational Titles 1
Drug testing 111

E

Education 60–61
Educational institutions 13
Educational requirements 3, 113
Employment agencies 12
Executive search 14
Extracurricular activities 62

F

Four–fifths rule 117

H

Hiring
 costs 21–22
 decisions 118, 125 – 127
Honesty tests 84

HOW TO HIRE WINNERS — LEGALLY

I

Interview
  examples 63–67
  preparation for 51–54
  principles 51
  samples of 63–67
Interviewers, training of 66
Impostors 46–49
Interest inventories 85

J

Job analysis 116
Job descriptions 3
Job fairs 13
Job posting 8
Job sample tests 87–88

L

Legal issues
  in recruitment 20–21, 106–107
  in applications 26–28, 105–106
  in interviewing 57, 107
  in physical examinations 109
  in testing 88–89

M

Managers 128
Military sources 13

N

Negligent hiring 20–21, 93, 116
Networking 8–9

O

Organizing for hiring decisions 125
Outplacement 14

INDEX

P

Person specifications 3, 7, 15
Personality 62–63
Physical examinations 109
Personality tests 83–84
Position descriptions 4, 5
Proficiency tests 82
Psychological tests 83–84, 112–113, 126

R

Records 116
Recruiting data bases 16–18
Recruiting techniques 8–15
References
   giving 102–103
   investigating 93–94
   investigating firms 100
   telephone reference guides 96
Résumés 35, 37–40
   analysis 41-49
Reverse discrimination 117

S

Sales representatives 28–33, 129
Sample interviews 69–77
Selection criteria 127–130
Senior citizens 13
Simulations 87–88

T

Testing 79–84
   aptitude 80–81
   honesty 84
   intelligence 80
   interests 85
   multiaptitude 81
   personality 83
   physical health 109
   proficiency 82
   sensory ability 82
   simulations 87–88
   special aptitudes 80-81

137

HOW TO HIRE WINNERS — LEGALLY

T

Test publishers 91–92
Test validation 119–120
Tests, buying 89–90

W

Walk–ins 9
Weighted application forms 45–46
Work experience 58–60, 115